Mc
Graw
Hill
Education

Cover and Title Page: Nathan Love

www.mheonline.com/readingwonders

Send all inquiries to:
McGraw-Hill Education
2 Penn Plaza
New York, New York 10121

ISBN: 978-0-02-131081-4
MHID: 0-02-131081-5

Printed in the United States of America.

2 3 4 5 6 7 8 9 QVS 20 19 18 17 16   B

ELD

My Language Book

Program Authors

Diane August

Jana Echevarria

Josefina V. Tinajero

Mc
Graw
Hill
Education

Unit 1

Week 4

Week 5

Unit 2

Week 4

Week 5

Unit 3   Unit Opener: **Changes Over Time** 84–85

Week 1

Week 2

Week 3

Unit 4

Week 4

Week 5

Unit 5

Week 4

Week 5

Unit 6

Getting to Know Us

The Big Idea

What makes you special?

Weekly Concept: At School

Essential Question
What do you do at your school?

Talk about the picture.
Circle what you like to do.

COLLABORATE

Weekly Concept: At School Guide children to name the activities they see in this classroom. Ask: *What are the children doing? What is the teacher doing?* Have children circle activities they like to do at school.

Have partners discuss and describe what they like to do at school, using this sentence frame: *At school I like to _____.* See Teacher's Edition p. 6 for scaffolded support with this page.

Talk about the pictures.
Draw what happens in your school.

COLLABORATE

Words and Categories: School Events Guide children to talk about the activities in the pictures. Help them name each activity. Ask: *What special things do you like to do at school?* Have children draw a school event they are looking forward to this year.

Have partners share and discuss their drawings. Offer these sentence frames to support discussion: *I look forward to _____.* *I like to _____.* See Teacher's Edition p. 9 for scaffolded support with this page.

A Talk about the pictures.

B Draw another wish from the story.

Respond to the Text: *This School Year Will Be the Best!* Guide children to talk about the pictures, and to retell the story. Then have them draw something else the students in the story wish for.

COLLABORATE

Have partners share and describe their drawings. Then have them discuss other things from the story that they would like to do this year. See Teacher's Edition p. 12 for scaffolded support with this page.

Talk about the picture.
Circle the tools you used today.

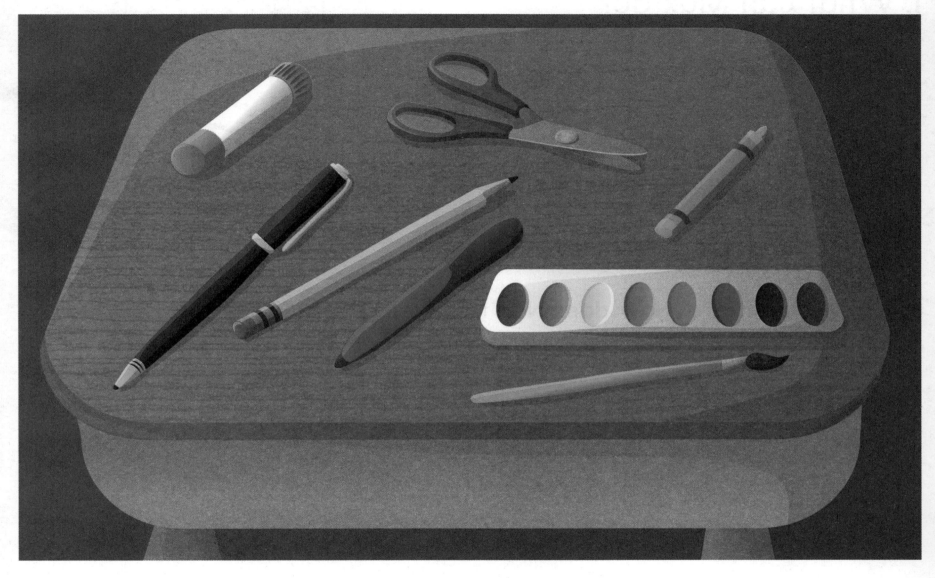

Oral Vocabulary: School Tools Guide children to name and talk about the tools in the picture. Ask: *Which tools do you use? What do you do with them?* Offer this sentence frame: *We use _____ to _____.* Have children circle tools they've used today.

Have partners discuss an activity they like to do in school, name the tools they use in that activity, and explain how to use those tools. See Teacher's Edition p. 16 for scaffolded support with this page.

A Answer the questions.

1. What can Max do?

_____

- -

_____

2. Why is Jack sad?

_____

- -

_____

B Draw a picture. How does Nan help?

Respond to the Text: ***Jack Can*** Review and retell the story with children. Read the questions and guide children to answer them. Then ask: *How does Nan help Jack? Why do you think she wants to help?* Have students draw their responses.

Have partners share their drawings and discuss the story using this sentence frame: *Nan helps Jack because* _____. See Teacher's Edition p. 19 for scaffolded support with this page.

Draw your ideas. Then, complete the sentences.

At First	Later

First, Jack feels _____ .

Then he feels _____ .

COLLABORATE

Writing Review the story *Jack Can* with children. Then, introduce the writing prompt: *How do Jack's feelings about school change?* Guide children to draw how Jack feels in each column, "at first" and "later". Then, guide them to complete the sentence frames.

Have partners share their drawings and sentences. Then have them explain how Jack's feelings change, using examples from the text. See Teacher's Edition p. 14 for scaffolded support with this page.

Draw a picture of where the six kids live.
Then complete the sentences.

Six kids live near _____ .

They _____ .

COLLABORATE

Writing Review *Six Kids*. Introduce the writing prompt: *Describe how where the six kids live affects what they do.* Have children draw a picture of where the six kids live. Ask: *What do they do there?* Then guide children to complete the sentences.

Have partners share their drawings with each other and read their complete sentences. Then have them show where they found their answer in the text. See Teacher's Edition p. 38 for scaffolded support with this page.

A Listen to the poem.
Circle the mixed-up sentences.

Miss Mixed-Up

Miss Mixed-Up mixed up her words.
She said, "I the birds see,"
not "I see the birds."
"My cat a tree is up!"
she cried one day.
What did she mean to say?

B Write the sentence in the correct order:
My cat a tree is up!

_____

- -

My cat _____ !

Read the story. Circle words with short _i_.

Bill at Bat

Bill is at bat.

Can Bill hit?

Yes! Bill can hit.

See it go up, up, up!

See it go down, down, down.

Bill did it. Go, Bill!

Fluency Read the story aloud and have children listen for your expression. Guide children to follow your example as they chorally read the story. Have them circle words with short _i_ and underline the high-frequency words _up_ and _down_.

Have partners read the story to each other. Have them change the name of the baseball player and read their new story aloud. See Teacher's Edition p. 50 for scaffolded support with this page.

Essential Question
What makes a pet special?

Talk about the picture.
Draw your favorite pet.

Weekly Concept: Our Pets Guide children to name and describe the animals they see. Ask: *Where are the girl and her mom? What are they looking at?* Have children talk about their favorite pet, and tell why they like it. Then have them add the animal to the pet store.

Have partners share their pictures and describe the features of the pets they drew, using this sentence frame: *My favorite pet has _____.* See Teacher's Edition p. 54 for scaffolded support with this page.

Compare the dogs. Then draw another dog.

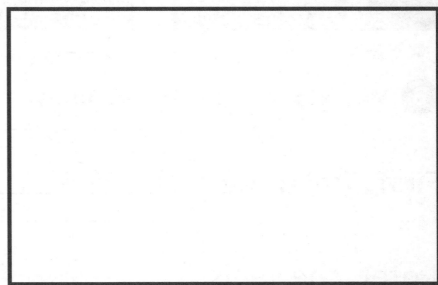

Words and Categories: Compare and Contrast Guide children to compare and contrast the dogs. Ask: *What color is each dog? What type of fur do they have? Are the tails the same or different?* Then have children draw a picture of another dog.

COLLABORATE

Have partners share their pictures, and talk together about how the two dogs are the same and different. See Teacher's Edition p. 57 for scaffolded support with this page.

A Talk about the pictures and the story.

B Write about Tinka's feelings.

First, Tinka feels _____ .

Later, she feels _____ .

COLLABORATE

Respond to the Text: *Cool Dog, School Dog* Review and retell the story with children. Have them describe what Tinka is doing in each picture, and tell how she feels. Then guide children to complete the sentence frames by writing a feeling word.

Have partners or small groups come up with rules for Tinka to follow at school. Ask groups to share their rules with the rest of the class. See Teacher's Edition p. 60 for scaffolded support with this page.

Name the pets and their things.
Draw lines to match them.

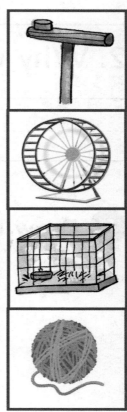

Oral Vocabulary: **Pet Supplies** Have children name each pet.
Ask: *What do these pets need?* Guide children to identify the pet
supplies, and to draw a line from each pet to its supplies. Have
children draw other items that pets need.

COLLABORATE

Have partners share their drawings of additional pet supplies, and
explain how each animal uses those objects. See Teacher's Edition
p. 64 for scaffolded support with this page.

Unit 1 • Week 3 • Oral Vocabulary   **21**

A Answer the questions.

1. What problem does Cliff have?

_____

- -

_____

2. Why is Slim a good pet?

_____

- -

_____

B Draw a picture. How does Slim help Cliff?

Respond to the Text: A Pig for Cliff Review and retell the story with children. Read the questions and guide children to answer them. Then have children draw their response showing how Slim helps Cliff.

Have partners share their answers and drawings with each other. Guide children to discuss reasons why Slim is a good pet, using evidence from the text. See Teacher's Edition p. 67 for scaffolded support with this page.

Draw a picture of Cliff and Slim.
Then write about it.

First, Cliff and Slim _____ .

Then, they _____ .

Writing Review *A Pig for Cliff* with children. Then introduce the writing prompt: *Write a new story for Cliff and Slim. How do they get into trouble? How do they get out of it?* Guide children to draw a picture of Cliff and Slim getting into trouble, and write about it.

Have partners describe their pictures and read their sentences to each other. Then have them ask and answer questions about how the characters get in and out of trouble in their new stories. See Teacher's Edition p. 62 for scaffolded support with this page.

Pets

Roses are red
Violets are blue
You have a pet
I want one, too

B Circle each statement.

The pets.   I have a cat.   I like dogs.   Like dogs.

Grammar: Statements Read the rhyme. Remind children that a statement is a sentence that tells something. Guide children to add correct punctuation to each statement. Then help children read the words at the bottom, and circle the statements.

Have partners work together to write other statements about the picture. Then have them present their statements to the group. See Teacher's Edition p. 73 for scaffolded support with this page.

Read the story. Circle words with *l*-blends.

Clap for Pigs

The pigs go up, up, up!

The pigs flip.

The pigs flop.

Will the pigs slip?

Come down, pigs!

The pigs do not slip.

The pigs are very good!

Clap for the pigs!

COLLABORATE

Fluency Read the story aloud, and discuss its meaning. Then read the story again, and have children repeat after you, copying your expression. Have children circle words with *l*-blends, and underline the high-frequency words *come* and *good*.

Have partners take turns reading the story to each other until they can read it fluently and with expression. See Teacher's Edition p. 74 for scaffolded support with this page.

Weekly Concept: Let's Be Friends

? **Essential Question**
What do friends do together?

Talk about the picture.
Draw more friends.

Weekly Concept: Let's Be Friends Have children talk about the picture. Ask: *Where are the children? What are they doing? Who is missing in the picture?* Have children draw the missing friends in each scene. Discuss how friends play together.

Have partners talk about ways they can play together, using these sentences frames: *We can _____ on the _____. We can _____ with the _____.* See Teacher's Edition p. 78 for scaffolded support with this page.

COLLABORATE

26 Unit 1 • Week 4 • Weekly Concept

Talk about the pictures. Draw a game you like.

1.

2.

3.

4.

(tl) Purestock/Getty Images; (tr) Lane Oatey/Blue Jean Images/Getty Images; (bl) Greatstock Photographic Library/Alamy

COLLABORATE

Words and Categories: Games Around the World Guide children to talk about what is happening in each picture. Ask: *How are these games like ones you play with your friends? How are they different?* Have children draw a favorite game in the last box.

Have children share their drawings with a partner and describe how to play the game they drew. Ask them to name the materials needed to play, and explain the rules. See Teacher's Edition p. 81 for scaffolded support with this page.

A Talk about the pictures.

B What do friends do?
Draw a picture.

COLLABORATE

Respond to the Text: *Friends All Around* Review and retell the story with children. Have them use the pictures to tell what friends do in the story. Then have children draw a picture of something else that friends do in the book.

Have partners share and describe their pictures, and talk about the friends in the book using this sentence starter: *Some friends like to* _____. See Teacher's Edition p. 84 for scaffolded support with this page.

28   Unit I · Week 4 · Respond to the Text: Big Book

Name the toys. Draw a toy you like.

COLLABORATE

Oral Vocabulary: Toys and Games Guide children to name each toy pictured. Have children talk about which games and toys they have played with, and tell how to play with them. Then invite them to draw their favorite toy or game.

Have partners share and describe the toy or game they drew. Then have them use sequence language to explain how to play with the toy or game. See Teacher's Edition p. 88 for scaffolded support with this page.

Unit 1 • Week 4 • Oral Vocabulary   **29**

A **Answer the questions.**

1. What do kids toss?

_____

_____

2. How do kids hop?

_____

_____

Jose Luis Pelaez/Getty Images

B **Draw a picture. What do kids make?**

COLLABORATE

Respond to the Text: ***Toss! Kick! Hop!*** Review and retell the story with children. Read the questions and guide students to answer them. Then have children draw a picture of what the kids make in the story.

Have partners share their drawings and discuss the story using these sentence frames: *The kids make* _____. *I know because I see* _____. See Teacher's Edition p. 91 for scaffolded support with this page.

Draw your ideas. Then, complete the sentence.

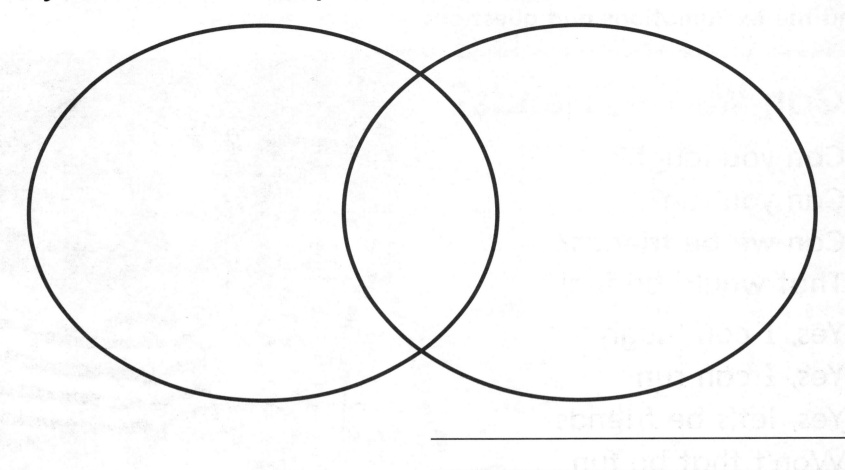

Playing soccer is the same as _____

_____

_____

_____ .

Writing Review *Toss! Kick! Hop!* Then introduce the writing prompt: *Look at the different things that the children are doing to have fun. How are they the same and different?* Have children draw soccer on one side of the Venn diagram, and another activity on the other.

Ask: *How are these activities the same?* Guide children to fill in the center of the diagram, and to complete the sentence. Then have partners discuss how the activities are the same and different. See Teacher's Edition p. 86 for scaffolded support with this page.

Listen to the rhyme.
Find the exclamations and questions.

Can We Be Friends?

Can you laugh?

Can you run?

Can we be friends?

That would be fun!

Yes, I can laugh

Yes, I can run

Yes, let's be friends

Won't that be fun

COLLABORATE

Grammar: Questions and Exclamations Read the rhyme, and have children repeat. Guide children to circle the first question in the rhyme and underline the first exclamation. Have them add a question mark or exclamation point to each sentence in the second stanza.

Have partners read the poem to each other. Then have them work together to write a new question and answer about friends, and present their new sentences to the group. See Teacher's Edition p. 97 for scaffolded support with this page.

Hero/Corbis/Glow Images

Read the story. Circle words with short *o*.

Flip, Flop, Fun

Jill will toss.

Bill hops up!

Will Bill miss?

Bill will toss, too.

It flips up!

It flops down.

Jill got it!

Fluency Read the story, and discuss its meaning. Point out your expression when you read questions and exclamations. Have children read the story chorally. Then have them circle words with short *o* and underline the high-frequency words *fun* and *too*.

COLLABORATE

Have children read the story to a partner. Then have pairs think of other questions they could ask about Jill and Bill. Have them practice asking and answering those questions. See Teacher's Edition p. 98 for scaffolded support with this page.

Weekly Concept: Let's Move!

? **Essential Question**
How does your body move?

Talk about the picture.
Draw yourself moving.

Weekly Concept: Let's Move! Guide children to name and talk about what they see in the picture. Ask: *What are these people doing? How are they moving their bodies?* Have children draw themselves moving in the scene.

COLLABORATE

Have small groups work together to brainstorm a list of ways that people move (*run, jump, hop, skip, etc.*). Ask groups to share their lists and act out the movements. See Teacher's Edition p. 102 for scaffolded support with this page.

Match the animals that move the same way.

COLLABORATE

Words and Categories: Alike and Different Guide children to name and talk about each animal. Have them match the animals that move the same way. Then have them say how the pairs of animals are alike and different.

Have partners think of another pair of animals and discuss how those two animals move, identifying how the animals are alike and different. See Teacher's Edition p. 105 for scaffolded support with this page.

A Talk about the pictures.
Draw an animal from the book.

B Write a sentence. Tell how the animal moves.

_____ _____

The _____ _____ .

Talk about how the kids move.
Then draw one more way to move.

(tl) Ken Karp/McGraw-Hill Education; (tc) Ingram Publishing/Alamy; (tr) Juice Images/Cultura/Getty Images; (bl) KOICHI SAITO/amanaimagesRF/Getty Images; (bc) RubberBall/SuperStock

COLLABORATE

Oral Vocabulary: Moving Words Guide children to name and describe how the children in the photos are moving. Then have them draw a person moving in a different way.

Have children work in small groups to take turns acting out movements as the remaining children describe what they are doing. See Teacher's Edition p. 112 for scaffolded support with this page.

A Answer the questions.

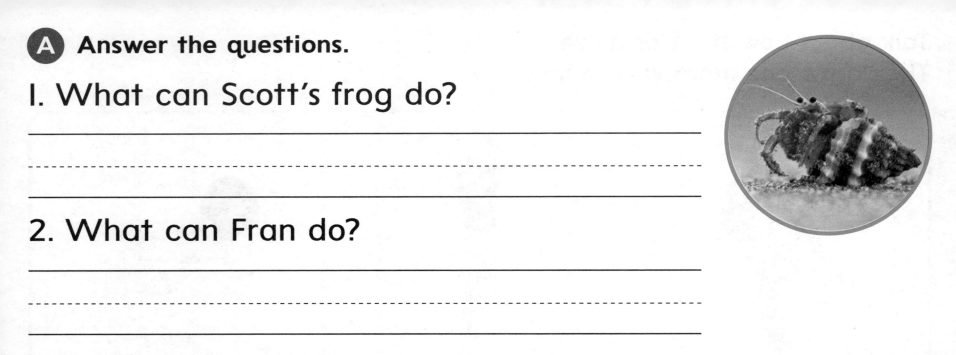

1. What can Scott's frog do?

_____

- -

_____

2. What can Fran do?

_____

- -

_____

B Draw a picture. How is Skip's crab like Skip?

COLLABORATE

Respond to the Text: _Move and Grin!_ Review and retell the story with children. Read the questions and guide children to answer them. Point out the way the author uses the text and the pictures to compare the animals to the children in the story.

Have partners choose one animal/child pairing from the story and talk about how they move in a similar way. See Teacher's Edition p. 115 for scaffolded support with this page.

Draw the steps of Fran's swimming motions.

First	Next

First, Fran _____ .

Next, she _____ .

Writing Review pages 98 and 99 of *Move and Grin!* Then, introduce the writing prompt: *Use first/next/then/last to describe the steps needed to make Fran's motions.* Guide children as they draw pictures of the first steps and complete the sentences.

Have partners read their sentences to each other. Then have them discuss what happens *then* and *last*, using text evidence to support their answers. See Teacher's Edition p. 110 for scaffolded support with this page.

A Listen to the poem. Circle the sentences.

Swim, swim, swim
Swish, swish, swish
In and out, over and under
I watched a lively fish.

Buzz, buzz, buzz
Fly, fly, fly
Higher and higher, up and away
I watched a fly glide by.

B Write a sentence.

_____

I watched _____ .

COLLABORATE

Grammar: **Writing Sentences** Read the rhyme, and discuss its meaning. Have children repeat. Guide children as they identify and circle the lines of the rhyme that are sentences. Ask: *What makes this a sentence?* Have children complete the sentence at the bottom.

Have partners read their sentences to each other, and work together to think of other sentences using the same pattern. Then have them share their new sentences with the group. See Teacher's Edition p. 121 for scaffolded support with this page.

Read the story. Circle words with *r-* and *s-* blends.

On the Grass

Come play with us.
We can play on the grass.
Fred will run and jump.
I will skip and flip.
You can move, too.
Can you spin and hop?
It is fun to play on the grass!

Fluency Read the story, modeling how to read with expression. Then ask volunteers to take turns reading each line. Have children circle words with *r-* and *s-* blends and underline the high-frequency words *jump*, *move*, and *run*.

COLLABORATE

Have partners take turns reading the story to each other until they can read it fluently. See Teacher's Edition p. 122 for scaffolded support with this page.

Unit 2
Our Community

The Big Idea

What makes a community?

Weekly Concept: Jobs Around Town

? Essential Question

What jobs need to be done in a community?

Talk about the picture.
Circle workers in the community.

Bakery

COLLABORATE

Talk about the pictures.
Draw your own stamp.

Words and Categories: Mail Words Guide students to talk about the pictures. Use the vocabulary *letter, envelope, address, mail carrier, deliver, stamp,* etc. Have children circle the mail carrier, and then draw their own stamp in the empty box.

Have partners share their stamps with each other and explain the significance of their designs. Have them talk about a time when they sent or received a piece of mail. See Teacher's Edition p. 135 for scaffolded support with this page.

How does Millie help the mail carrier?
Draw a picture. Then write.

Millie helps by _____

Respond to the Text: *Millie Waits for the Mail* Guide children to
retell the story. Ask: *At the beginning of the story, what is Millie's
favorite part of the day?* Then have children draw a picture and write
about how Millie helps the mail carrier at the end of the story.

Have partners describe their favorite part of the story, using this
sentence starter: *I liked the beginning/ end because* _____.
See Teacher's Edition p. 138 for scaffolded support with this page.

46   Unit 2 • Week I • Respond to the Text: Big Book

Talk about the pictures.
Match the tools to the person who uses them.

COLLABORATE

Oral Vocabulary: Job Tools Guide children to identify and talk about the construction worker and doctor. Ask: *What does this person do? What does this tool do?* Help them name each tool and match the tools to the person who uses them.

Have partners brainstorm other jobs and tools. Then have them act out the jobs, showing how each worker uses the tools. See Teacher's Edition p. 142 for scaffolded support with this page.

A Answer the questions.

1. Where do Ben and Mom go?

_____

- -

_____

2. How does the vet help?

_____

- -

_____

B Draw a picture. What workers does Ben see?

COLLABORATE

Respond to the Text: **Good Job, Ben!** Review and retell *Good Job, Ben!* with children. Read the questions and guide children to answer them. Have children draw two or three of the workers that Ben sees.

Have partners share their answers and drawings with each other. Then have them describe the job of each worker they drew, using evidence from the text. See Teacher's Edition p. 145 for scaffolded support with this page.

Draw or write about the jobs.
Then, finish the sentence.

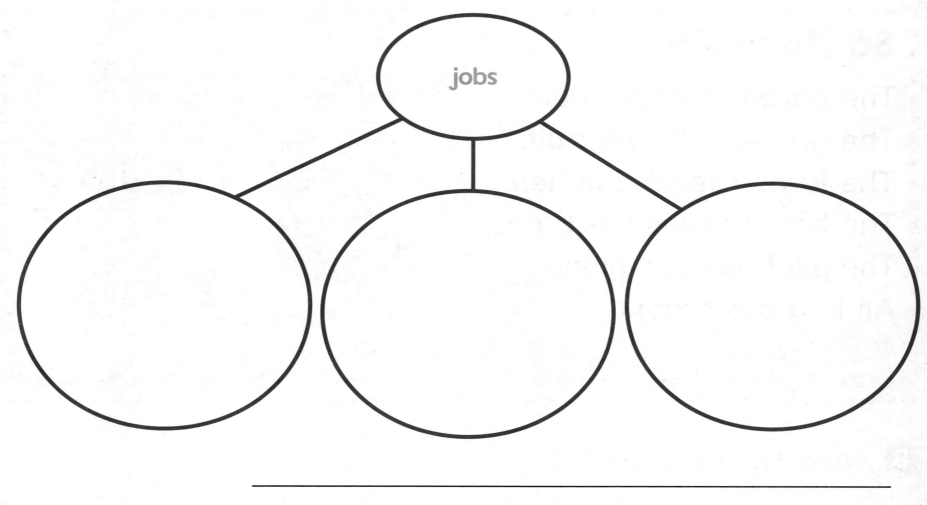

I want to be a _____.

Writing Review *Good Job, Ben!* with children. Then, introduce the writing prompt: *Which job in* Good Job, Ben! *would you like to have? Why?* Have children use the web to draw or write about three jobs. Then have them choose their favorite, and complete the sentence.

COLLABORATE

Have partners discuss the reasons why they are interested in that job, using evidence from the text. Offer this sentence frame: *I want to be a _____ because _____*. See Teacher's Edition p. 140 for scaffolded support with this page.

Talk about the picture.
Circle and count the animals.

Words and Categories: **Cardinal and Ordinal Numbers** Help children name the animals, and have them circle the groups of animals by type. Then guide them to count the animals and discuss their positions using ordinal numbers such as *first, second,* and *third.*

Have partners ask and answer questions about the number of animals and their position, such as: *How many ducks are there? Which turtle is first in line?* See Teacher's Edition p. 183 for scaffolded support with this page.

A Talk about the pictures.
Then draw a bayou baby.

B How does the mom help the baby you drew?

_____

- -

_____

COLLABORATE

Respond to the Text: _Babies in the Bayou_ Review and retell the Big Book with children. Ask children to name the animals in the pictures, and tell how the mothers help their babies. Then have them draw an additional bayou baby from the book, and answer the question.

Have partners share their drawings, and read their sentences to each other. Then have them act out a scene between a bayou baby and its mother. See Teacher's Edition p. 186 for scaffolded support with this page.

Circle animals that live in the ocean.
Then draw them in an ocean scene.

Oral Vocabulary: Animal Habitats Guide children to name the animals and talk about their habitats. Ask: *Where does a crab live? Where does a cow live?* Then have children circle animals that live in the ocean and draw them in an ocean scene.

Have partners share their drawings. Then have them compare and contrast the ocean habitat with a cow's or giraffe's habitat. See Teacher's Edition p. 190 for scaffolded support with this page.

A Answer the questions.

I. What animal is in the grass?

_____

- -

_____

2. What animal hunts?

_____

- -

_____

B Draw a picture. Show where ants live.

COLLABORATE

Universal Stopping Point Photography/Flickr/Getty Images

Respond to the Text: *The Best Spot* Review and retell the selection with children. Have children name the animals in the selection, and discuss where they live. Then read the questions and guide children to answer them.

Have partners share their answers and pictures with each other. Then have them discuss three things they learned about forest animals from reading the selection. See Teacher's Edition p. 193 for scaffolded support with this page.

Draw and write about park animals.

Page 1	Page 2

A _____ lives _____ .

_____

It eats _____ .

COLLABORATE

Writing Introduce the writing prompt: *Use* The Best Spot *as a model and write the first two pages of an informative text about animals that live in a park.* Guide children to draw and write their ideas. Then have them complete the sentences about a park animal.

Have partners share their ideas and read their sentences to each other. Have them ask and answer questions about animals that live in a park. See Teacher's Edition p. 188 for scaffolded support with this page.

Listen to the poem.
Circle the possessive nouns.

A Forest Home

The bird's nest,
the owl's tree,
the bee's hive,
look and see!

The raccoon's log,
the bug's ground,
the duck's pond,
all safe and sound!

COLLABORATE

Grammar: Possessive Nouns Read the poem, and discuss its meaning. Read it again, and have children repeat. Guide children to find and circle the possessive nouns. Then have children ask and answer questions about ownership, e.g.: *What belongs to the bird?*

Have partners work together to write new sentences about other animals, using this sentence frame: *This is the _____'s _____.* Then have them present their sentences to the group. See Teacher's Edition p. 199 for scaffolded support with this page.

Read the story. Circle words with end blends.

Good Bug!

Look at the bug run past!

It runs in the mud.

It runs in the sand.

It runs under the step.

It is a fast bug.

Now, the bug must rest.

The bug must eat.

Do it again, bug!

Fluency Read the story and discuss its meaning. Then do a choral reading, having children mimic your reading rate. Point out end punctuation and commas. Have children circle words ending with *-st* and *–nd,* and underline the high-frequency words *under* and *eat.*

Have partners take turns reading the story to each other until they can read it fluently. Remind them to pay attention to end punctuation. See Teacher's Edition p. 200 for scaffolded support with this page.

Weekly Concept: Let's Help

? Essential Question
How do people help out in the community?

Circle the people who are helping.
Talk about how they help.

COMMUNIT
CENTER

COLLABORATE

Weekly Concept: Let's Help Guide children to talk about the picture. Ask: *What are the children doing? How are they helping the community?* Have children circle the people who are helping and tell about a time they helped in a similar way.

Have partners explain why each pictured activity is important, using this sentence frame: _____ *is important because* _____.
Have partners explain whether or not they agree, and why.
See Teacher's Edition p. 204 for scaffolded support with this page.

Talk about the pictures. Then draw your own.

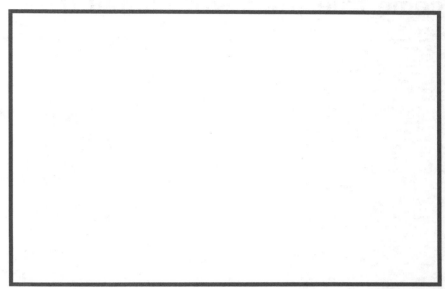

Words and Categories: Fair and Equal Discuss what is happening in each picture. Ask: *What is unfair, here? Who is being excluded, or left out?* Have children re-draw the situations to show everyone being treated fairly and equally.

Have partners discuss times when they have felt excluded or when they were being treated unfairly. See Teacher's Edition p. 207 for scaffolded support with this page.

Draw how Martin Luther King Jr.'s dream came true. Then write about it.

Martin dreamed _____

_____

_____

COLLABORATE

Respond to the Text: *The Story of Martin Luther King Jr.* Review and retell the Big Book with children. Ask: *What was Martin's dream?* Have children draw a picture showing an example of how Martin's dream came true, and then write about it.

Have partners talk about the pictures that they drew, and read their sentences to each other. Then have them share their favorite part of the book. See Teacher's Edition p. 210 for scaffolded support with this page.

70 Unit 2 • Week 4 • Respond to the Text: Big Book

Talk about the pictures.
Then draw yourself helping.

donate

recycle

paint

COLLABORATE

Oral Vocabulary: Volunteering Point to each picture, read the labels, and guide children to talk about what the volunteers are doing. Have children draw a picture of how they have helped or would like to help in their community.

Have partners share their drawings, and talk about an activity they would like to do to help in the community using this sentence frame: *I would like to* _____. See Teacher's Edition p. 214 for scaffolded support with this page.

A Answer the questions.

1. Why do the rabbits say hush?

_____

_____

2. What is the little rabbits' problem?

_____

_____

B Draw a picture. How does Thump Thump help?

Respond to the Text: **Thump Thump Helps Out** Review and retell the story with children. Discuss Thump Thump's character and his role in the story. Then read the questions and guide children to answer them.

Have partners share their answers and drawings with each other. Then have them talk about other ways Thump Thump could help. See Teacher's Edition p. 217 for scaffolded support with this page.

Draw or write your ideas. Then write a sentence.

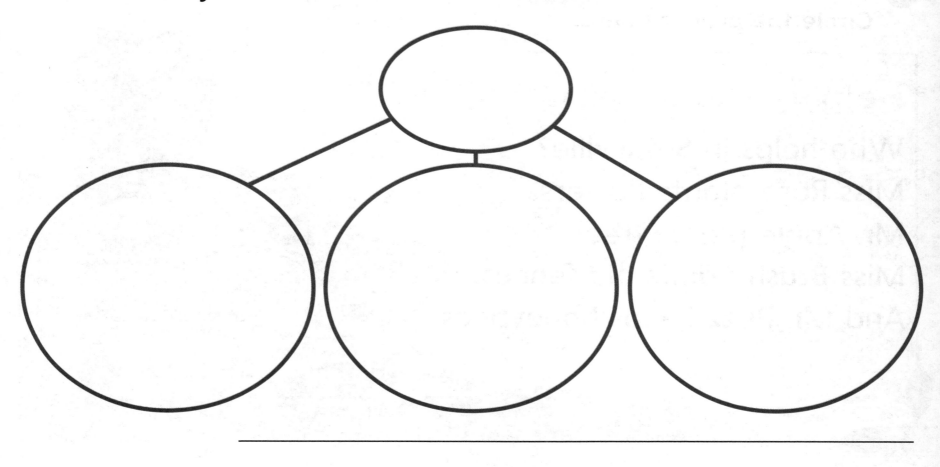

My character _____

_____

_____ .

Writing Introduce the writing prompt: *Use* Thump Thump Helps Out *as a model to write a fantasy about a character who has an unusual habit.* Explain what a habit is. Have children draw or name their character in the top oval, and draw or write details in the others.

Have children complete the sentence about their character. Then have partners tell each other a story about their character and his/her unusual habit. See Teacher's Edition p. 212 for scaffolded support with this page.

Unit 2 • Week 4 • Writing   **73**

A Listen to the rhyme.
Circle the proper nouns.

Helping Hands Around Town

Who helps in Smallville?
Miss Rose plants flowers.
Mr. Apple plants trees.
Miss Brush paints old fences.
And Mr. Buzz keeps honeybees.

B Write two common nouns.

_____   _____

- - - - - - - - - - - - - - -   - - - - - - - - - - - - - - -

_____   _____

COLLABORATE

Grammar: **Common and Proper Nouns** Read the rhyme and discuss its meaning. Read it again, and have children repeat. Guide children as they circle each proper noun, and underline the common nouns. Then, have children write two common nouns from the rhyme.

Have children work together to think of a proper noun and common noun for a pet and a place, and use them in sentences. See Teacher's Edition p. 223 for scaffolded support with this page.

Read the story. Circle words with *th, sh,* and *-ng*.

Beth and Seth

Beth and Seth like to help.

Beth picks up the trash.

Seth brings the sack.

They help with lots of things.

Do you want to help them?

Just call Beth and Seth!

COLLABORATE

Fluency Read the story aloud and discuss its meaning. Tell children to listen for the changes in your voice when you read the question and exclamation. Then have children read chorally. Have them circle words with *th, sh* and *-ng* blends and underline the word *want*.

Have partners take turns reading the story to each other until they can read it fluently. Remind them to change their voices when they read the question and exclamation. See Teacher's Edition p. 224 for scaffolded support with this page.

? Essential Question

How can you find your way around?

Talk about the pictures.
Draw a path between the houses.

Your house

Your friend's house

COLLABORATE

Weekly Concept: Follow the Map Guide children to talk about the map, locating different places. Ask: *What does the map show you? What places do you see?* Have children circle *Your house* and *Your friend's house,* and then mark the route between the houses.

Have children draw squares around two other places on the map. Have them explain to a partner how to get from one place to the other. See Teacher's Edition p. 228 for scaffolded support with this page.

76 Unit 2 • Week 5 • Weekly Concept

Talk about the pictures.
Draw two things from your bedroom.

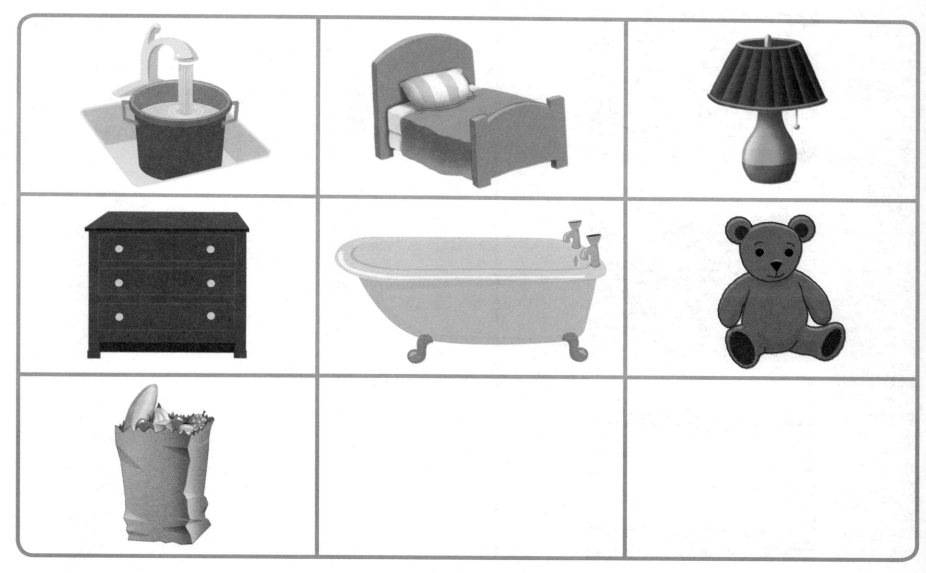

 COLLABORATE

Words and Categories: Bedroom Items Guide children to name and talk about each item. Ask: *In what room in the house can you find this?* Have children circle items that can be found in a bedroom. Then have them draw two things from their bedroom.

Have partners ask and answer questions about the items they drew. Then have them describe their own bedrooms, using adjectives to add more detail. See Teacher's Edition p. 231 for scaffolded support with this page.

A Circle the map of a country.   # B Draw a map from the book.

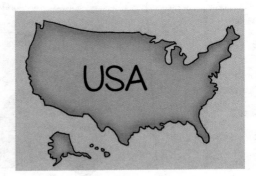

USA

Topeka ☆

K A N S A S

Respond to the Text: *Me on the Map* Review and retell the Big Book with children. Discuss each type of map. Ask: *What does the map show?* Have students circle the map of a country, and compare it to the other maps. Then have them draw another map from the book.

COLLABORATE

Have partners discuss the maps that they drew, using this sentence frame: *This is a map of _____.* Guide them to tell what they included on their map, and why. See Teacher's Edition p. 234 for scaffolded support with this page.

Talk about the picture. Draw yourself playing.

COLLABORATE

Oral Vocabulary: Prepositions Guide children to talk about the picture using prepositions. Ask: *Is the sandbox above or below the slide? Is the pond near to or far from the tree? Which things can you go on top of/ inside of?* Have children draw themselves playing.

Have partners show each other their drawings and talk about what they like to do at the playground. Guide them to use prepositional phrases in their explanations. See Teacher's Edition p. 238 for scaffolded support with this page.

A Answer the questions.

1. Why do the kids use a map?

_____

- -

_____

2. What place is by a lake?

_____

- -

_____

B Draw a place from the town map.

COLLABORATE

Respond to the Text: **Which Way on the Map?** Review and retell the selection with children, discussing how the map helps Mitch and Steph find their way. Read the questions and guide children to answer them. Have children draw a place from the town map.

Have partners share and discuss their drawings with each other. Then have them look at the town map in the selection, and locate the places they drew. See Teacher's Edition p. 241 for scaffolded support with this page.

Draw and write your ideas.

Photographs	Maps

Writing Review *Which Way on the Map?* Then introduce the writing prompt: *Why does the author use both photographs and parts of the map? What does this help a reader to understand?*

Guide children to complete the chart with reasons why the author uses photographs and maps. Then have partners share their completed charts and ideas with each other. See Teacher's Edition p. 236 for scaffolded support with this page.

Unit 2 • Week 5 • Writing **81**

A Listen to the rhyme.
Circle the plural nouns.

To the Cheese Shop

Two mice went for a walk.
One mouse wore a cap,
the other did not.
They ran to the cheese shop,
quick on their feet.
One foot after the other,
to get a cheese treat!

B Write the plurals.

_____   _____

mouse _____   foot _____

Grammar: Irregular Plural Nouns Read the rhyme and discuss its meaning. Read it again and have children repeat. Help children circle the irregular plural nouns in the rhyme. Then have children write the irregular plural nouns in the spaces provided.

COLLABORATE

Have partners work together to create the plural form of the nouns *child, man,* and *woman,* and use the plurals in sentences. See Teacher's Edition p. 247 for scaffolded support with this page.

Read the story. Circle words with blends.

Lunch by the Pond

Let's go for a walk.

We will bring the map.

Let's look for a place to play.

We can play catch.

We can sit under the branch.

We can eat lunch.

Crunch, munch, yum!

We will have such fun!

Fluency Read the story and discuss its meaning. Ask: *What should I do with my voice at the end of the last sentence?* Have children read the story chorally. Then have them circle words with *ch* and *-tch* blends, and underline the high-frequency words *walk* and *place*.

Have partners take turns reading the story to each other until they can read it fluently. Remind them to read the exclamations with expression. See Teacher's Edition p. 248 for scaffolded support with this page.

Unit 2 • Week 5 • Fluency **83**

Changes Over Time

The Big Idea

What can happen over time?

Weekly Concept: What time is it?

Essential Question
How do we measure time?

Talk about the pictures. Circle the clocks.

Weekly Concept: Time Guide children to talk about the pictures. Ask: *What time of day is it in each picture?* Discuss what the family does in the morning and at night. Have children circle the clocks and discuss how they can be used to tell time.

Have partners talk about what they do at certain times of the day, using this sentence frame: *At _____ o'clock, I _____.* See Teacher's Edition p.258 for scaffolded support with this page.

Talk about the calendar. Circle one day.

October

Sunday	Monday	Tuesday	Wednesday	Thursday	Friday	Saturday
			1	2	3	4
5	6 *Dentist appointment*	7	8	9	10	11 *GAME*
12	13	14	15	16 *Jane's Birthday*	17	18
19	20	21	22	23	24	25
26	27	28	29	30	31 *School picnic*	

Words and Categories: Calendars Guide children to identify the parts of the calendar. Explain that the whole grid is one month, the highlighted boxes show one week, and a single box is one day. Have students circle one day. Ask: *Which day of the week is the picnic?*

COLLABORATE

Have partners work together to add a new appointment to the calendar. Have them name the day of the week and the date of the appointment. See Teacher's Edition p. 26I for scaffolded support with this page.

A Draw something that takes one second, one minute, and one hour.

1.

2.

3.

B What can you do in an hour? Write about it.

In an hour, I can _____

_____

_____

_____

_____ .

Respond to the Text: A Second is a Hiccup Review and retell the book with children. Help them find examples in the text of what one can do within each time frame (e.g. second, minute, hour). Then guide children to draw and write their answers.

COLLABORATE

Have partners share their drawings and read their writing to each other. Then ask them to discuss what they can do in a day and a week. See Teacher's Edition p. 264 for scaffolded support with this page.

88 Unit 3 · Week I · Respond to the Text: Big Book

Talk about the pictures.
Draw what you do at night.

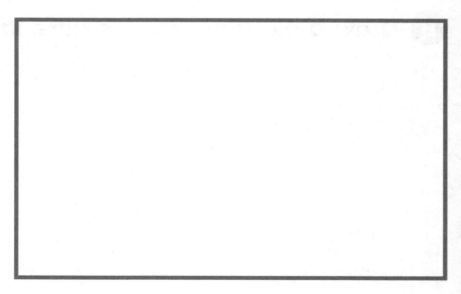

COLLABORATE

Oral Vocabulary: *Times of day* Point to each picture and ask children what is happening, and when. Ask: what happens *early/ late* in the day? Have them use the words: *in the morning, at noon,* and *at night,* and then draw a picture of something they do at night.

Have partners share and describe their drawings. Then have them ask each other whether they would rather be up *early* in the morning or stay up *late* at night. Have them describe their favorite time of day. See Teacher's Edition p. 268 for scaffolded support with this page.

A Answer the questions.

1. What makes Nate late first?

_____

- -

_____

2. What else makes Nate late?

_____

- -

_____

B Draw a picture. What is Nate late for?

Respond to the Text: *Nate the Snake Is Late* Review and retell the story with children. Ask: *Why is Nate late?* Have children describe the stops Nate makes that cause him to be late. Read the questions and guide children to write and draw their answers.

Have partners share their pictures and explain to each other why Nate doesn't want to be late, using this sentence starter: *Nate doesn't want to* _____. See Teacher's Edition p. 271 for scaffolded support with this page.

Draw or write your ideas for two new pages.

First new page	Second new page

Writing Review *Nate the Snake is Late* with children. Then introduce the writing prompt: *Add two pages to the story to tell what happens next.* Guide children to draw or write their ideas for the new pages.

COLLABORATE Have partners share their drawings with each other and tell what happens in their new pages. Then have children work together to write rhyming sentences for their new story pages. See Teacher's Edition p. 266 for scaffolded support with this page.

A Listen to the rhyme. Circle the verbs.

We Grow Older

We hear the clock.
We count the days.
Time moves in many ways.
We watch the sun rise.
We turn the calendar page.
We celebrate our new age!

B Write two verbs from the poem.

_____   _____
-     -
_____   _____

COLLABORATE

Grammar: Verbs Read the rhyme, and discuss its meaning. Then reread, and have children echo-read. Remind children that a verb is an action word. Guide children to find and circle the verbs. Then have them write two verbs from the rhyme on the lines.

Have partners work together to write new sentences for two verbs from the rhyme. Then have them present their sentences to the group. See Teacher's Edition p. 277 for scaffolded support with this page.

Read the story. Circle words with long _a_.

A Fun Day!

Today is a fun day!
We make hats. We eat cake.
We run and jump and spin.
Why must it end now?
It is late. Mom and Dad
must rest!

Fluency Read the story, demonstrating how to read exclamations and questions. Then have children chorally read the story, copying your expression. Have children circle long _a_ words spelled _a_e_ and underline the high-frequency words _today_, _why_, and _now_.

COLLABORATE

Have partners read the story to each other until they can read it fluently. Then have them ask and answer questions about what happened on the fun day, based on the text and picture. See Teacher's Edition p. 278 for scaffolded support with this page.

Weekly Concept: Watch It Grow!

? Essential Question
How do plants change as they grow?

Talk about the pictures. Draw a tree.

seeds

seedlings

young tree

COLLABORATE

Weekly Concept: Watch It Grow! Guide children to name and talk about what they see in the pictures. Read the labels with children, and discuss the steps in growing and caring for a tree. Then have children draw a full-grown tree.

Have partners discuss what the children do to help the tree grow, using these sentence frames: *First, the boy* _____. *Then, the girl* _____. See Teacher's Edition p. 282 for scaffolded support with this page.

Talk about the pictures.
Draw a vegetable or fruit of the same color.

Words and Categories: Vegetables and Fruits Guide children to name the vegetables and fruits. Discuss with them how each grows and which parts we eat. Then have children draw another fruit or vegetable of the same color in each row.

Have partners name and describe the fruits and vegetables that they drew. Then have them work together to list three purple or yellow fruits or vegetables. See Teacher's Edition p. 285 for scaffolded support with this page.

A Circle the Mystery Vine.

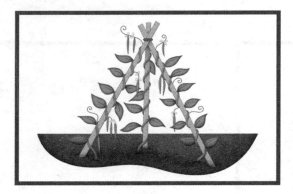

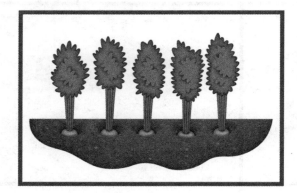

B What grows on the Mystery Vine? Draw a picture.

Respond to the Text: *Mystery Vine* Review and retell the story with children. Have children circle the picture that shows the mystery vine. Then have them orally complete this sentence frame and draw the corresponding picture: *The mystery vine grows _____.*

Have partners talk about what the family in the story does with their pumpkins, using this sentence frame: *The family makes _____.* See Teacher's Edition p. 288 for scaffolded support with this page.

Talk about the pictures.
Draw a growing plant.

Oral Vocabulary: Growing Plants Guide children to name and talk about the pictures in the picture bank. Ask children to describe the steps of growing a plant. Have them use objects from the picture bank to draw a growing lemon plant.

COLLABORATE

Have partners share their drawings and describe what plants need to grow, using this sentence frame: *A plant needs* _____. See Teacher's Edition p. 292 for scaffolded support with this page.

Unit 3 • Week 2 • Oral Vocabulary **97**

A Answer the questions.

I. How does Mike help plant?

_____

- -

_____

2. What plan does Gramps have?

_____

- -

_____

B Draw a picture. What does the family grow?

COLLABORATE

Respond to the Text: _Time to Plant!_ Review and retell the story
with children. Read the questions and guide children to write their
answers. Have children draw a picture of the vegetables that the
family grows.

Have children act out the play in small groups, with each child
taking a part. Then have partners tell each other their favorite part
of the story. See Teacher's Edition p. 295 for scaffolded support with
this page.

Draw your ideas for a new page. Then write.

Beth: _____

Mike: _____

Writing Review *Time to Plant!* Introduce the writing prompt: *Add a page at the end of the story in which the kids tell Miss White what they did to grow the plants.* Have children draw their ideas for a new page, and write what Beth and Mike say.

Have partners share their drawings, and discuss their ideas for the new page. Then have them read and act out their new sentences. See Teacher's Edition p. 290 for scaffolded support with this page.

A Listen to the poem. Circle the verbs.

Planting Treats

Jan digs a hole for tiny seeds.

Jan plants the seeds, and pulls the weeds.

Jan waters her plant for many weeks.

And now her tree gives yummy treats!

B How does the tree grow?

_____

First, Jan _____ .

_____

Then, Jan _____ .

Read the story. Circle words with long *i*.

The Plant

Jim: This plant will not grow!

Dad: Do you water it?

Jim: Yes, many times a day.

Dad: Does the sun shine on it?

Jim: Yes, it shines a lot.

Dad: Then it will grow. You will see!

Jim: I wish I could see a
pretty plant today!

Fluency Read the story. Divide the class into two groups and read chorally, with one group reading as Jim and the other as Dad. Guide children to circle the long *i* words spelled *i_e* and underline the high-frequency words *grow*, *water*, and *pretty*.

Have partners read the story, trading off so that each takes both parts. Then have them extend the story by writing what Dad and Jim say after the plant grows. See Teacher's Edition p. 302 for scaffolded support with this page.

? **Essential Question**
What is a folktale?

Talk about the picture.
Circle the animal character.

Once Upon A Time,

Weekly Concept: Tales Over Time Guide children to talk about
Little Red Riding Hood and discuss what they know about folktales.
Remind them that folktales have been told for many years, and often
have animal characters. Have children circle the animal character.

COLLABORATE

Have partners name and discuss another folktale they know, telling
each other about the characters and the story. See Teacher's Edition
p. 306 for scaffolded support with this page.

102 Unit 3 • Week 3 • Weekly Concept

Use the pictures to tell the story.
Circle the characters.

Words and Categories: Folktales Guide children to use the pictures to tell the story of Little Red Riding Hood. Ask: *Who are the characters? Where does the story happen? What happens?* Have children name and circle the characters.

COLLABORATE

Have partners or small groups discuss the plot, setting, and characters of the story. Then have them work together to act out the story. See Teacher's Edition p. 309 for scaffolded support with this page.

A Circle the last story Papa reads.

B Why does the chicken interrupt?

_____

- -

The chicken _____ .

COLLABORATE

Respond to the Text: _Interrupting Chicken_ Review and retell the story with children. Have them circle the picture that shows the last folktale Papa reads. Ask: _How does the little chicken feel about the stories?_ Guide children to answer the question.

Have partners read their answers to each other. Then have them work together to tell the story of one folktale pictured above. See Teacher's Edition p. 312 for scaffolded support with this page.

104 Unit 3 • Week 3 • Respond to the Text: Big Book

Use the pictures to tell the story.
Draw the ending.

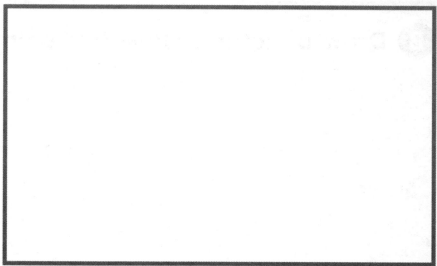

Oral Vocabulary: Telling a Story Use the pictures to tell the story of The Gingerbread Man. Ask: *What happens first? What happens next? What happens last?* Have children tell and draw the ending.

Have partners tell about their favorite part of The Gingerbread Man, using this sentence starter: *My favorite part of the story is _____.* Then have them explain why they like that part. See Teacher's Edition p. 316 for scaffolded support with this page.

A Answer the questions.

1. Why does the rabbit like the mitten?

_____

- -

_____

2. What animal goes in the mitten last?

_____

- -

_____

B Draw a picture. Show two animals in the mitten.

Respond to the Text: *The Nice Mitten* Review and retell the folktale with children. Guide children to identify the animals, in order, that go into the mitten. Then have them answer the questions and draw a picture. Ask: *Why do the animals in your picture like the mitten?*

Have partners share their drawings with each other. Then have them discuss why they did or didn't like the ending of the folktale. See Teacher's Edition p. 319 for scaffolded support with this page.

Draw your ideas. Then, complete the sentences.

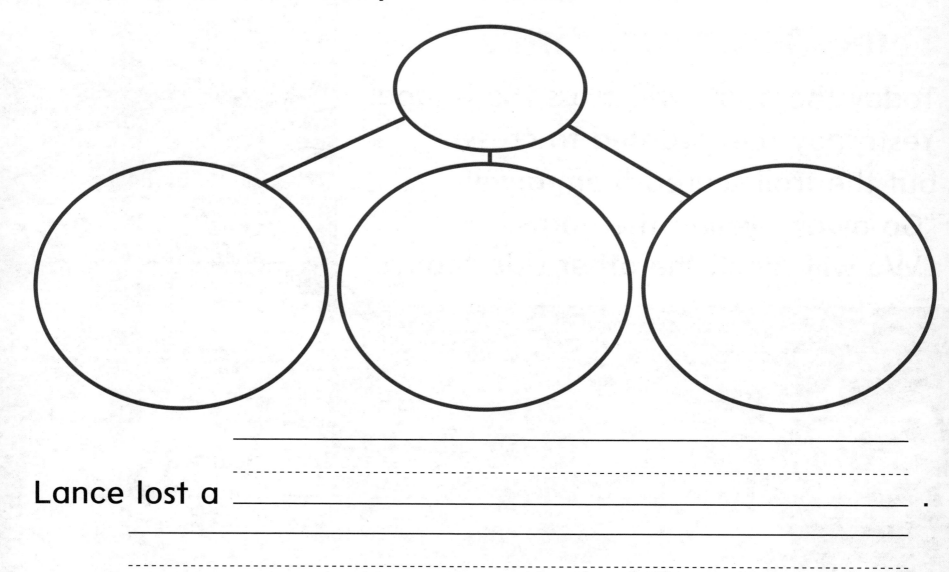

Lance lost a _____ .

Then, _____ .

Writing Review the *The Nice Mitten* with children. Then introduce the writing prompt: *Rewrite the story so that the boy loses a jacket, sock, or hat instead of a mitten.* Have them draw the lost item in the top circle, and then draw and write the events that happen next.

Have partners share their ideas and tell their new stories to each other. Then have them ask and answer questions about how their new story is similar to and different from the original. See Teacher's Edition p. 314 for scaffolded support with this page.

Read the story. Circle past-tense verbs.

Three Billy Goats Gruff

Today the goats will cross the bridge!
Yesterday they wanted to cross,
but the troll scared them away.
"Go away," yelled the goats.
"We will reach the other side today!"

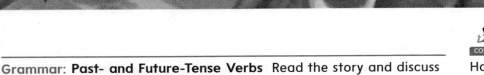

COLLABORATE

Read the story.
Circle words with soft _c_ and _g_.

Midge's Cave

Once upon a time,
there was a fox named Midge.
She wanted a nice place to live.
So she went up on a ridge.
She looked around.
There was a nice cave!
This place made her happy!

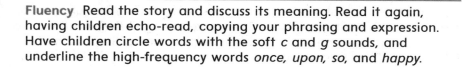

Fluency Read the story and discuss its meaning. Read it again, having children echo-read, copying your phrasing and expression. Have children circle words with the soft _c_ and _g_ sounds, and underline the high-frequency words _once, upon, so,_ and _happy._

Have partners read the story to each other. Remind them to read with expression, and to show excitement when reading the exclamations. See Teacher's Edition p. 326 for scaffolded support with this page.

? Essential Question
How is life different than it was long ago?

Talk about the pictures.
Circle the tools used to clean.

Then

Now

COLLABORATE

Weekly Concept: Now and Then Guide children to talk about the pictures. Ask: *What are the children doing? How are the activities the same? How are they different?* Have children circle the tools used to clean. Then help them name and describe each tool.

Have partners talk about the differences between the lives of the children in the two pictures. Then have them tell their partner a story about how one of the children helps at home. See Teacher's Edition p. 330 for scaffolded support with this page.

Talk about the pictures.
Draw another train car.

Words and Categories: Railroad Words Guide children to name and discuss the images in the first row: *tracks, station, engineer.* Then discuss the train cars in the second row: *passenger car, caboose.* Have children draw another train car.

Have partners pretend to be an engineer and a passenger. Have them act out a scene involving those two characters. See Teacher's Edition p. 333 for scaffolded support with this page.

A Talk about the pictures.

B How do people travel now?

_____

- -

Now people _____

_____

_____

- -

_____ .

COLLABORATE

Respond to the Text: *The Last Train* Guide children to use the pictures to review and retell *The Last Train*. Ask: *Why did the train stop running?* Then, have children talk about the new kinds of transportation on pages 28-29, and answer the question.

Have partners read their answers to each other and explain how transportation has changed from long ago to now, using evidence from the text. See Teacher's Edition p. 336 for scaffolded support with this page.

Talk about the pictures. Then draw.

COLLABORATE

Oral Vocabulary: **Technology** Guide children to talk about each picture and compare the old technology with the new. Ask: *How is the new technology different from the older versions?* Then, have children draw themselves using one type of new technology.

Have partners share their drawings and explain the purpose of the technology they drew, using this sentence frame: *I am using _____ to _____.* See Teacher's Edition p. 340 for scaffolded support with this page.

A Answer the questions.

1. How is cooking different today?

_____

_____

2. How were homes different in the past?

_____

B Draw a picture. How do kids help out at home today?

Respond to the Text: *Life at Home* Review and retell *Life at Home* with children. Guide them to answer the questions. Then, have children draw an example of how kids help out at home today, such as cleaning up or helping to prepare food.

Have partners share their drawings with each other. Then, have them compare and contrast how kids help at home today with how they helped in the past. See Teacher's Edition p. 343 for scaffolded support with this page.

Draw or write your ideas.
Then, complete the sentences.

In the Past	Now

_____

- -

In the past, people _____ .

_____

- -

Now, people _____ .

Writing Review *Life at Home* with children. Introduce the writing prompt: *Based on* Life at Home, *do you think home life is better now, or was it better in the past? Why?* Guide children to draw or write their ideas in the organizer and complete the sentences.

Have partners read their completed sentences to each other. Then have them share their opinions using this sentence frame: *I think home life is _____ now because _____*. See Teacher's Edition p. 338 for scaffolded support with this page.

COLLABORATE

A Listen to the poem. Circle the verbs *is* and *are*.

Dinner Time

Our home is cozy.
Our kitchen is bright.
The pots are hot.
Dad made dinner tonight!
The table is set.
We are ready to eat at last.
Dinner time is special,
today and in the past.

B Complete the sentences.

One pot _____ hot. Two pots _____ hot.

COLLABORATE

Grammar: *Is* and *Are* Read the poem and discuss its meaning. Read it again and have children repeat. Remind them that *is* and *are* are present-tense verbs, meaning they tell what is happening now. Guide children to circle *is* and *are*. Then have them complete the sentences.

Have partners read their completed sentences. Then have one partner create and share a new sentence using the verb *is*. Have the other partner change the sentence to use *are*. See Teacher's Edition p. 349 for scaffolded support with this page.

Read the story. Circle words with _u_e_ and _o_e_.

Jump Rope

Do you like jumping games?
Jumping rope is an old game.
Boys and girls made up the
game long ago.
They made up cute songs.
Today, kids still jump rope.
Kids around the globe play
the game!

COLLABORATE

Fluency Read the story aloud, and discuss its meaning. Then have children read the story chorally. Have them circle words with long _o_ spelled _o_e_ and long _u_ spelled _u_e_, and underline the high-frequency words _old_, _boys_, _girls_, and _ago_.

Have partners take turns reading the story to each other until they can read it fluently. Then have them tell why they do or don't enjoy jumping rope. See Teacher's Edition p. 350 for scaffolded support with this page.

? **Essential Question**
How do we get our food?

Talk about the picture. Draw lines from the foods at the farm stand to the pizza.

COLLABORATE

Weekly Concept: From Farm to Table Guide children to name and describe the foods at the farm stand: fresh mozzarella, onions, mushrooms, etc. Then have children draw a line connecting each of the foods at the farm stand to the toppings on the pizza.

Have partners describe the foods at the farm stand, and identify which they have tried. Then have them say which toppings they would put on their own pizza. See Teacher's Edition p. 354 for scaffolded support with this page.

Talk about the pictures.
Draw a food made from milk.

(tl) irin-k/age fotostock; (tc) Ingram Publishing/Alamy; (tr) Jacques Cornell/McGraw-Hill Education; (cl) Jacques Cornell/McGraw-Hill Education; (c) Tadeusz Wejkszo/iStock/360/Getty Images; (cr) Ingram Publishing/SuperStock; (bl) Ingram Publishing/SuperStock; (bc) Photographer's Choice/Getty Images

COLLABORATE

Words and Categories: Ingredients Guide children to name and talk about each ingredient on the left, and the foods made from it. Ask: *What foods are made from wheat? What is made from apples?* Have children draw another food made from milk.

Have partners share their drawings and describe the food made from milk. Then have them name other ingredients and the foods made from them. See Teacher's Edition p. 357 for scaffolded support with this page.

A Talk about the pictures.

1.

2.

3.

B Write about the foods.

1. _____

2. _____

3. _____

COLLABORATE

Respond to the Text: *Where Does Food Come From?* Have children name the foods (rice, popcorn, egg) and talk about where they come from. Then have them write a sentence about each food's origins, using this sentence frame: *The _____ come(s) from a _____.*

Have partners share their sentences. Then have them use the sentence frame to build sentences about where other foods come from. See Teacher's Edition p. 360 for scaffolded support with this page.

Talk about the pictures.
Draw your favorite meal.

breakfast

lunch

dinner

COLLABORATE

Oral Vocabulary: Meals of the Day Talk about each picture with children. Discuss the foods eaten at each time of day and the places where we eat them. Ask: *What do you eat for breakfast/ lunch/ dinner/ snacks?* Have children draw a picture of their favorite meal.

Have partners share their drawings and talk about why they like their favorite meal, using details. Have partners respond by saying why they do or don't agree. See Teacher's Edition p. 364 for scaffolded support with this page.

A **Answer the questions.**

1. What is bread made from?

_____

- -

_____

2. What is jam made from?

_____

- -

_____

GlowImages/Alamy

B **Choose one food from the story.**
How is it made? Draw a picture.

COLLABORATE

Respond to the Text: *A Look at Breakfast* Review and retell the selection with children. Ask: *What is the boy eating for breakfast?* Read the questions and guide children to answer them. Have them draw a picture of how one food from the story is made.

Have partners share their answers and drawings with each other. Then have them discuss three things they learned about how the breakfast foods in the selection are made. See Teacher's Edition p. 367 for scaffolded support with this page.

Draw and write your ideas.

1.

(writing lines)

before

2.

(writing lines)

after

Writing Review *A Look at Breakfast*. Then introduce the prompt: *Choose one set of pages. Would you rather have the original item or the finished product? Why?* Have children draw and write about one item and finished product.

COLLABORATE

Have partners share their drawings and writing. Then have them tell which of the two foods they would rather have, and explain their choice. See Teacher's Edition p. 362 for scaffolded support with this page.

A Listen to the rhyme. Circle the contractions. Then write them below.

Who Will Help?

"Who will help me bake the bread?"
asked the Little Red Hen.
"I can't help," said the Pig.
"It isn't my job," said the Cat.
"It doesn't seem right," said the Dog.
"Then don't ask for a bite!" said Hen.

B can + not   is + not   does + not   do + not

_____   _____   _____   _____

- -

_____   _____   _____   _____

COLLABORATE

Grammar: Contractions with *not*. Read the rhyme, and discuss its meaning. Then reread, and have children repeat. Guide them to circle the contractions with *not*. Ask: *What two words make up this contraction?* Have children write the contractions on the lines.

Guide partners to work together to write new sentences that use contractions with *not*. Then, have them present their sentences to the group. See Teacher's Edition p. 373 for scaffolded support with this page.

Read the story. Circle words with *-ook* and *-ood*.

We Bake Bread

My mom and I like to bake bread.
We look in a cook book.
We mix and mix.
Then, we bake the bread.
Soon, the bread is done.
It was a lot of work.
But it is good!

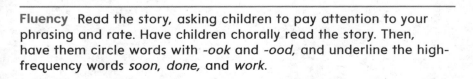

Fluency Read the story, asking children to pay attention to your phrasing and rate. Have children chorally read the story. Then, have them circle words with *-ook* and *-ood*, and underline the high-frequency words *soon, done,* and *work.*

Have partners take turns reading the story to each other until they can read it fluently. Remind children to pause at commas and periods. Then have them tell the steps to make bread, using the text. See Teacher's Edition p. 374 for scaffolded support with this page.

Animals Everywhere

The Big Idea

What animals do you
know about?
What are they like?

? Essential Question

How do animals' bodies help them?

**Talk about the picture.
Draw one more animal.**

COLLABORATE

Weekly Concept: Animal Features Guide children to name and describe each animal and its features. Ask: *How does this animal move? What body parts help it? How?* Have children circle important body parts of each animal, and draw another ocean animal.

Have partners describe the animals they drew, and talk about each animal's features using this sentence frame: *The _____ uses its _____ to _____ .* See Teacher's Edition p. 384 for scaffolded support with this page.

A Use the picture to talk about the story.

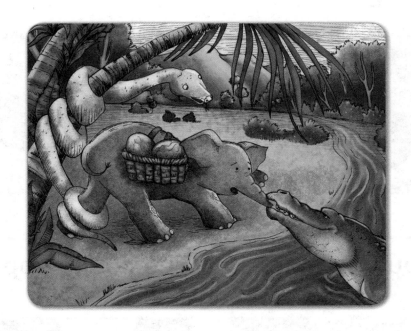

B Why is a long nose better for the elephant?

_____

The elephant _____

_____

_____

Respond to the Text: "The Elephant's Child" Guide children to use the picture to review and retell the story. Ask: _Why does the elephant go to the crocodile? What does he learn?_ Then, have children answer the question.

Have partners read their answers to each other. Then have them discuss other uses for a long nose, using this sentence frame: _The elephant can use his nose to_ _____. See Teacher's Edition p. 387 for scaffolded support with this page.

Look at the picture. Read the word. Then read the sentence.

proud

She feels proud about winning.

chop

The cook chops the food.

swayed

The trees swayed in the wind.

signal

His hand signal shows he is happy.

COLLABORATE

Vocabulary: *A Tale of a Tail* Read each word and sentence, and have children repeat. Talk about the photos, and explain how the words relate to each image. Provide other contexts for each word. Ask: *When have you felt proud? What else can you chop?*

Have children circle the vocabulary words in the sentences. Then have partners write a new sentence for each vocabulary word, and draw pictures to illustrate their ideas. See Teacher's Edition p. 391 for scaffolded support with this page.

Draw and write your ideas.

Frog's voice is croaky because _____

_____

_____ .

COLLABORATE

Writing Review *A Tale of a Tail* with children. Then, introduce the writing prompt: *Write a tale explaining why the frog has a croaky voice.* Ask: *What happens to the frog to make its voice croaky?* Have children draw and write their ideas for a new tale.

Have partners read their sentences and tell their tale to each other. Have them provide useful feedback to their partner, using this sentence frame: *I like your tale because* _____. See Teacher's Edition p. 392 for scaffolded support with this page.

Talk about the animals. Then, draw one more.

1.

2.

3.

COLLABORATE

Oral Language: Animal Features Guide children to talk about the features that the animals in each row share, and how these features help the animal move and/or protect itself. Then, have children draw an animal with the same features as the others in the third row.

Have partners share their drawings and tell which body parts their animal shares with a horse and a sheep, using this sentence frame: *A horse, a sheep, and a _____ all have _____.* See Teacher's Edition p. 394 for scaffolded support with this page.

A **Answer the questions.**

1. Why is Ray upset about his tail?

_____

- -

_____

2. Why do Ray's friends come running?

_____

- -

_____

B **Why is Ray's flat tail better than his fluffy tail?**

_____

- -

_____

- -

_____

COLLABORATE

Respond to the Text: *A Tale of a Tail* Review and retell the story with children. Read the questions and guide children to write their answers. For the last question, ask them to find the passage in the text that supports their answer.

Have partners share their answers with each other and explain their thinking. Have them use text evidence to persuade each other that a flat tail is better than a fluffy tail. See Teacher's Edition p. 397 for scaffolded support with this page.

Draw an animal finding food.
Then, write about it.

Writing Review *Go Wild!* with children. Then introduce the writing prompt: *How do animals use their body parts to help them find food?* Have children draw an animal from the selection, circling the body parts that help it find food. Then have them write about it.

COLLABORATE

Have partners share their drawings and read their writing to each other. Then have them use details to explain to their partner how the animal they drew uses its body parts to find food. See Teacher's Edition p. 440 for scaffolded support with this page.

Unit 4 • Week 3 • Writing   147

Talk about the pictures.
Draw a pet and a wild animal eating.

COLLABORATE

Oral Vocabulary: **Pets and Wild Animals** Help children name each animal and say if it is a pet or wild, or both. Discuss the differences between the two environments. Have children draw a pet eating in the kitchen, and a wild animal eating in the forest.

Have partners share and explain their drawings. Have them discuss the differences between how pets and wild animals find food and survive. See Teacher's Edition p. 442 for scaffolded support with this page.

A Answer the questions.

1. How do squirrels find food?

_____

\- -

_____

2. What animals eat both plants and animals?

_____

\- -

_____

B Choose an animal. Tell how it finds food.

_____

\- -

_____

\- -

_____

Alex Fieldhouse/Alamy

COLLABORATE

Respond to the Text: *Go Wild!* Review and retell the selection with children. Read the questions and guide children to write their answers. For the last question, invite children to locate the passage in the text that supports their answer.

Have partners read their answers to each other. Then have them explain how the animal they wrote about survives in the wild, using this sentence frame: *A _____ survives by _____ .* See Teacher's Edition p. 445 for scaffolded support with this page.

A **Listen to the poem.**
Circle *go*, *went*, *do* and *did*.

Go to Sleep

Yesterday the bears did a lot.

They ate berries in a sunny spot.

They went fishing, and then they ran.

Today they have a different plan.

They go to their cave, and they go to sleep.

They do not come out for a week!

B **Write about the bears. Use *go*, *went*, *do*, or *did*.**

_____

- -

The bears _____ .

COLLABORATE

Grammar: **Go and Do** Read the poem aloud, and discuss its
meaning. Reread and have children repeat. Then have children circle
went, *go*, *did* and *do*, and complete the sentence about the bears
using one of the verbs.

Have partners work together to write new sentences using *do, did,
go,* and *went.* Have them present their sentences to the group. See
Teacher's Edition p. 451 for scaffolded support with this page.

Read the story. Circle words with long o.

Toad and Goat

Toad and Goat wanted to find food,
so they went over the road.
Goat spotted big, yellow plants.
Toad spotted big, black bugs.
"I like big, yellow plants,"said Goat.
"I like big, black bugs," said Toad.
Goat and Toad ate until the sun was low.

Fluency Read the story to children, and discuss its meaning. Then ask volunteers to echo-read after you, copying your phrasing. Have children circle words with long o and underline the high-frequency words *find*, *food*, and *over*.

Have partners take turns reading the story to each other until they can read it fluently. Remind them to pause after a period, and to read with expression. See Teacher's Edition p. 452 for scaffolded support with this page.

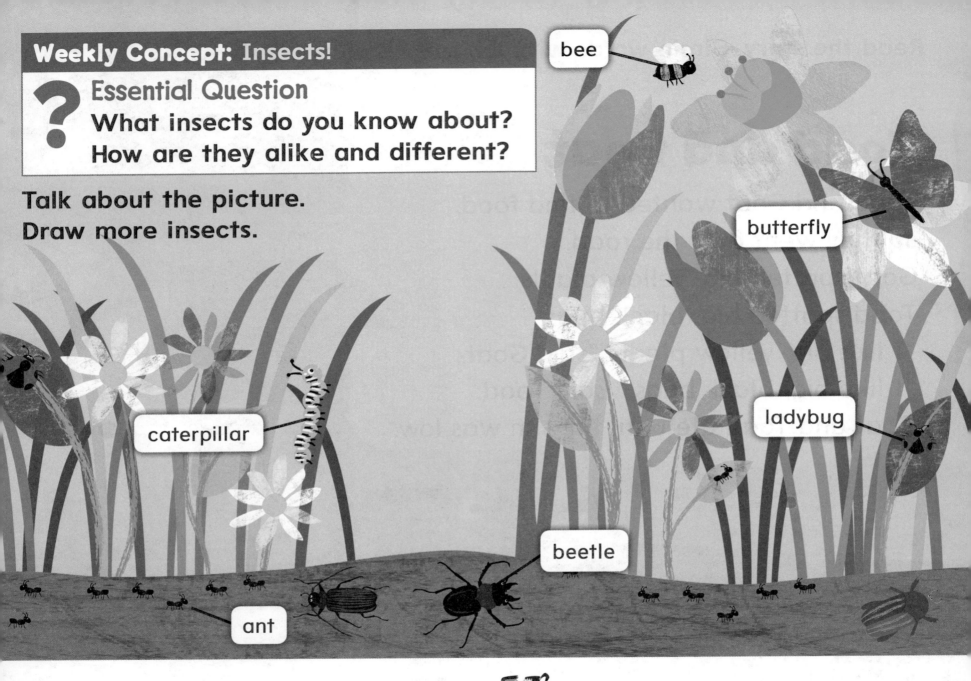

Weekly Concept: Insects!

? Essential Question

What insects do you know about? How are they alike and different?

Talk about the picture.
Draw more insects.

bee

butterfly

ladybug

caterpillar

beetle

ant

COLLABORATE

Weekly Concept: Insects! Point to and read the labels. Guide children to talk about and compare the insects. Ask: *Which insects can fly? Which insects move on the ground? How do the insects eat?* Have children draw more insects in the picture.

Have partners share their drawings and tell which kind of insects they drew. Then have them compare and contrast their new insects with the ones in the picture. See Teacher's Edition p. 456 for scaffolded support with this page.

A Use the pictures to answer the question.

B How does an insect's shape and color help it?

An insect's shape and color help it to _____

_____

_____ .

Respond to the Text: "Insect Hide and Seek" Guide children to use the photos to review and retell the selection. Ask: *Why are the insects hard to see on the plants? How does this help them?* Then read the question and have children complete the sentence.

COLLABORATE

Have partners read their answers to each other. Then have them compare the pictured insects using this sentence frame: *Both insects _____ .* See Teacher's Edition p. 459 for scaffolded support with this page.

(l) Creatas Images/PictureQuest; (r) Creatas Images/PictureQuest

Look at the picture. Read the word. Then read the sentence.

chat

Friends chat about their day.

dash

The dogs dash to get the ball.

creep

A snail creeps along slowly.

cheer up

The balloons cheer up the kids.

COLLABORATE

Vocabulary: *Creep Low, Fly High* Read each word and sentence, and have children repeat. Talk about the photos, and explain how the words relate to each image. Provide other contexts for each word. Ask: *What do you like to chat about? What cheers you up?*

Have children circle the vocabulary word in each sentence. Then have partners create a new sentence for each vocabulary word, and draw pictures to illustrate their ideas. See Teacher's Edition p. 463 for scaffolded support with this page.

Draw or write your ideas.
Then, complete the sentences.

At the beginning	At the end

_____

- -

At the beginning, Caterpillar _____ .

_____

- -

At the end, Caterpillar _____ .

Writing Review *Creep Low, Fly High* with children. Then, introduce the writing prompt: *How do Caterpillar's feelings change from the beginning to the end of the story?* Have children draw or write about Caterpillar, and then complete the sentences.

Have partners share their ideas and sentences with one another. Then have them use sequence words to tell how Caterpillar's feelings change. See Teacher's Edition p. 464 for scaffolded support with this page.

Talk about the pictures.
Then, draw one more insect.

stinger

antenna

wing

leg

shell

COLLABORATE

Oral Vocabulary: Insect Body Parts Read each label with children and talk about the insect body parts. Ask: *Which body part might hurt people? Which body part protects the insect? Which parts help an insect move?* Then, have children draw another insect.

Have partners share their drawings with each other. Have them explain the body parts they included and how they are used. See Teacher's Edition p. 466 for scaffolded support with this page.

A Answer the questions.

1. What do the bugs boast about?

_____

- -

_____

2. Why are the bugs worried?

_____

- -

_____

B What happens to Caterpillar? Write about it.

_____

- -

_____

- -

_____

Respond to the Text: *Creep Low, Fly High* Review and retell the story with children. Read the questions and guide children to answer them. Ask: *What did you already know about caterpillars and butterflies? What new information did you learn?*

Have partners share their answers with each other, and find evidence in the text to support their answers. Then have them describe how a caterpillar turns into a butterfly. See Teacher's Edition p. 469 for scaffolded support with this page.

Listen to the rhyme. Circle *see* and *saw*.

I See Wings!

Yesterday I saw ladybugs
sitting on the grass.
Today I see another one,
through a magnifying glass!

Yesterday I saw the spots.
Today I can see the wings.
When I look up close,
I see all kinds of things!

COLLABORATE

Grammar: *See* and *Saw* Read the rhyme, and discuss its meaning. Reread and have children repeat. Explain that *see* means "look at now," and *saw* means "looked at in the past." Have children circle the present tense and past tense of *see*.

Have partners compose new lines of poetry, using these sentence frames: *Yesterday, I saw _____. Today, I see _____.* Then have them present their new lines to the group. See Teacher's Edition p. 475 for scaffolded support with this page.

Read the story. Circle words with long _i_.

No Bug Bites!

My pal and I were on a step at night.
A bug flew under the light.
"I know this is not a fly," I said.
"It might try to bite my leg!"
Then the bug flew our way,
so I caught that bug and sent it away!

COLLABORATE

Fluency Read the story to children, and explain its meaning. Then ask volunteers to echo-read after you, copying your expression. Have children circle words with long _i_ sound spelled _y, i,_ and _igh,_ and underline the high-frequency words _were, flew, know,_ and _caught._

Have partners take turns reading the story to each other until they can read it fluently. Remind them to show emotion when they come to an exclamation mark. See Teacher's Edition p. 476 for scaffolded support with this page.

Weekly Concept: Working with Animals

? Essential Question
How do people work with animals?

Talk about the picture.
Circle animals that help people.

COLLABORATE

Weekly Concept: Working with Animals Guide children to name the animals in the picture and talk about what is happening. Ask: *What are the animals doing? How is the cat different from other animals in the picture?* Have children circle animals that are helping people.

Have partners discuss the picture by taking turns asking and answering questions about how people work with the guide dog, the horse, and the fire dog. See Teacher's Edition p. 480 for scaffolded support with this page.

160 Unit 4 • Week 5 • Weekly Concept

A Use the picture to answer the question.

B Why does Chung's dog dance for him?

_____

- -

Chung's dog dances because _____

_____

- -

_____ .

COLLABORATE

Respond to the Text: **"Ming's Teacher"** Use the picture to review and retell the story with children. Ask: _What is Chung doing? What is Chung's dog doing? What does Ming want to do?_ Guide children to read the question and write their answer.

Have partners read their answers to each other. Then have them discuss what Ming learns about how to work with animals. See Teacher's Edition p. 483 for scaffolded support with this page.

Look at the picture. Read the word.
Then read the sentence.

buddy

A buddy is a good friend.

fussy

The baby is tired and fussy.

traffic

This street has a lot of traffic.

raise

The parents raise their son.

COLLABORATE

Vocabulary: *From Puppy to Guide Dog* Read each word and sentence, and have children repeat. Talk about the photos, and explain how the words relate to each image. Provide other contexts for each word. Ask: *Who is your buddy? Who is raising you?*

Have children circle the vocabulary word in each sentence. Then have partners create a new sentence for each vocabulary word, and draw pictures to illustrate their ideas. See Teacher's Edition p. 487 for scaffolded support with this page.

Draw and write your ideas.
Ask and answer questions about guide dogs.

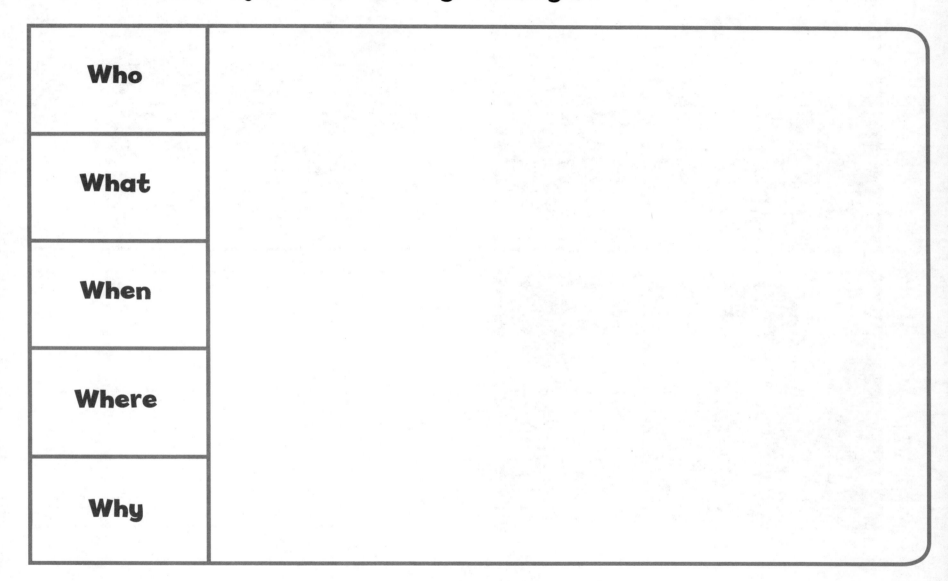

Who	
What	
When	
Where	
Why	

COLLABORATE

Writing Review *From Puppy to Guide Dog* with children. Introduce the writing prompt: *Based on pages 104-106, what should a guide dog do well after being trained? Use text evidence.* Guide children to draw and write their ideas about what guide dogs should do well.

Have partners ask and answer *W* questions about their ideas, such as: *What should guide dogs know how to do? Why do they need to be able to do those things? Who do they help?* See Teacher's Edition p. 488 for scaffolded support with this page.

Talk about the pictures. Draw a dog helper.

1.

2.

3.

4.

COLLABORATE

Oral Vocabulary: **Dog Helpers** Guide children to talk about each picture. Ask: *What is this dog's job? How does the person in the picture work with the dog? What skills does the dog need to do a good job?* Have children draw a picture of another dog helper.

Have partners tell each other about their drawings and explain how the dog is helping the person, using this sentence frame: *The dog is helping by _____ .* See Teacher's Edition p. 490 for scaffolded support with this page.

A Answer the questions.

1. Who teaches a puppy to be a guide dog?

_____

- -

_____

2. How do guide dogs help people?

_____

- -

_____

B How does a puppy become a guide dog?
Write about it.

_____

- -

_____

- -

_____

COLLABORATE

Respond to the Text: *From Puppy to Guide Dog* Review and retell the selection with children. Read the questions to children and guide them to write their answers. For the last question, ask children to locate the passages in the text that support their answers.

Have partners share their answers with each other. Then have them work together to tell how a puppy becomes a guide dog, using sequence language. See Teacher's Edition p. 493 for scaffolded support with this page.

Listen to the poem.
Circle words that tell when.

My Dog

Yesterday, I found a dog.
Today, he stayed with me.
Soon, I will teach him a trick.
Then, he'll never leave!

First, I pet him and scratch his back.
Next, I give him treats.
Later, my dog will impress
everyone he meets!

Grammar: Adverbs That Tell When Read the rhyme, and discuss its meaning. Reread and have children repeat. Guide children as they find and circle words that tell when an action takes place: *yesterday, today, soon, then, first, next,* and *later.*

Have partners write a story about a dog using the adverbs *first, next, then,* and *last.* Have them present their story to the group. See Teacher's Edition p. 499 for scaffolded support with this page.

Read the story. Circle words with long *e*.

My Buddy Benny

This is Benny. He is my buddy.
He works hard to help me.
He leads me and keeps me safe.
When Benny is near me, I feel happy.
He is my buddy. He would
read a book to me if he could!

COLLABORATE

Fluency Read the story aloud. Have children listen for changes in your expression as you read, and then chorally read the story with you. Have children circle words with *long e* spelled *-y*, and underline the high-frequency words *hard, near,* and *would.*

Have partners read the story to each other. Remind them to pause at periods and to show emotion at the final exclamation. Then have partners describe what Benny does to help. See Teacher's Edition p. 500 for scaffolded support with this page.

Figure It Out

The Big Idea
How can we make sense of the world around us?

Weekly Concept: See It, Sort It

? Essential Question
How can we classify and categorize things?

Talk about the picture.
Then, sort the clothes.

COLLABORATE

Weekly Concept: See It, Sort It Guide children to talk about the scene, naming the types of clothing and discussing the sizes and colors. Then have children choose one grouping (hats, shirts, red or yellow items, etc.) and draw it in on the empty table.

Have partners share their drawings and explain the characteristics they used to sort the items. Then have them discuss other ways they could sort the clothes. See Teacher's Edition p. 510 for scaffolded support with this page.

A Use the picture to answer the question.

B Why do the three bears have different chairs and beds?

_____

- -

The bears have different chairs and beds _____

_____

- -

_____ .

COLLABORATE

Look at the picture. Read the word. Then read the sentence.

thick

A thick jacket keeps you warm.

floppy

The dog has floppy ears.

yarn

She is making a hat with yarn.

grab

He grabs the apple to pick it.

COLLABORATE

Vocabulary: *A Barn Full of Hats* Read each word and sentence and have children repeat. Talk about the photos, and explain how the words relate to each image. Provide other contexts for each word. Ask: *When do you use a thick blanket? What else is made with yarn?*

Have children circle the vocabulary word in each sentence. Then have partners write a new sentence for each vocabulary word, and draw pictures to illustrate their ideas. See Teacher's Edition p. 517 for scaffolded support with this page.

Draw your ideas. Then, write.

This hat is just right because _____

Writing Review *A Barn Full of Hats* with children. Then, introduce
the writing prompt: *Did each of the animals choose the right hat?
Why or why not?* Have children choose one animal and draw it with
its hat. Then have them complete the sentence.

COLLABORATE

Have partners share their work, and offer opinions about the animals'
hats using text evidence, and this sentence frame: *The* _____
did / didn't choose the right hat because _____. See Teacher's
Edition p. 518 for scaffolded support with this page.

Draw a picture that belongs in each row.

1.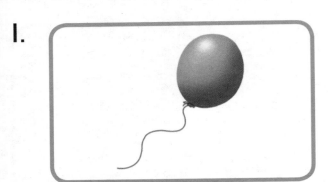

2.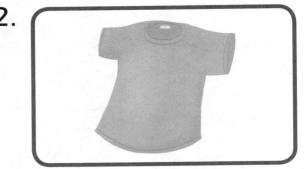

3.

COLLABORATE

Oral Vocabulary: Shape, Color, Texture Guide children to name the items in each row and to discuss their shape, color, and texture. Provide adjectives as needed. Ask: *How are the pictures alike?* Have children draw another object in each category (round, blue, bumpy).

Have partners share their drawings and explain why the objects they drew belong in the row. Then have them name additional objects that belong in each category. See Teacher's Edition p. 520 for scaffolded support with this page.

A Answer the questions.

1. What kinds of hats are in the box?

_____

- -

_____

2. How does the hen plan to use her hat?

_____

- -

_____

B What is the best kind of hat for Horse? Write about it.

_____

- -

_____

- -

_____

COLLABORATE

Respond to the Text: *A Barn Full of Hats* Review and retell the story with children. Read the questions and guide children to answer them. For the last question, invite children to locate the passage in the text that supports their answer.

Have partners read their answers to each other. Then have them work together to build on the story and tell a new ending, in which the animals all switch hats. See Teacher's Edition p. 523 for scaffolded support with this page.

A **Answer the questions.**

1. Why did Takahashi start building robots?

_____

- -

_____

2. Why did he change the way robots walked?

_____

- -

_____

B **What kinds of things can his robots do?**
Write about it.

_____

- -

_____

- -

_____

Respond to the Text: *The Story of a Robot Inventor* Review and
retell the selection with children. Ask: *How did Takahashi use his
imagination to create something new?* Read the questions and guide
children to answer them. Remind them to use text evidence.

COLLABORATE

Have partners read their answers to each other. Then have them
offer opinions about which of Takahashi's inventions is the best, and
explain why. See Teacher's Edition p. 571 for scaffolded support with
this page.

A Listen to the poem. Circle comparing words.

Towers and Bridges

Cole's tower is tall,
but Sara's is taller,
and Diego's is the tallest of all.
Henry's bridge is small,
but Oscar's is smaller,
and Nina's is the smallest of all.

B Write two words that compare.

_____   _____

- - - - - - - - - - - - - - -   - - - - - - - - - - - - - - -

_____   _____

COLLABORATE

Grammar: **Adjectives that Compare** Read the poem, and discuss its meaning. Reread, and have children repeat. Then have children circle the adjectives that compare, and underline the endings in the words that tell us they are comparisons: *-er* and *-est*.

Have partners work together to write new sentences for the poem using *big, bigger,* and *biggest*. Then have them present their new sentences to the group. See Teacher's Edition p. 577 for scaffolded support with this page.

Read the story. Circle words with *or* and *ore*.

An Old Phone

Look at this old phone.

It was made before you were born.

Can you guess how to use it?

You use your finger to dial.

Then you speak.

Make sure to plug in the cord,

or the phone won't work.

Do you think today's phones are better?

Why or why not?

Fluency Read the story to children, and discuss its meaning. Then have children echo-read after you. Have children circle words with *or* and *ore*, and underline the high-frequency words *guess, sure*, and *better*.

Have partners answer the question at the end of the story, and persuade their partners that today's phones are or aren't better than the old phone. See Teacher's Edition p. 578 for scaffolded support with this page.

Weekly Concept: Sounds All Around

? Essential Question
What sounds can you hear?
How are they made?

Talk about the picture.
Circle things that make sounds.

COLLABORATE

Weekly Concept: Sounds All Around Guide children to name what they see in the scene and talk about the sounds: birds chirping, wind, rustling leaves, musical sounds, human voices, and transportation sounds. Have children circle things in the scene that make sounds.

Have partners describe the sounds being made in the scene, and discuss when they have heard similar sounds. Then have them categorize the sounds into two groups: loud and quiet sounds. See Teacher's Edition p. 582 for scaffolded support with this page.

A Use the picture to answer the question.

B Why do the parents bring in the animals?

_____

The parents think _____

_____

_____ .

COLLABORATE

Respond to the Text: "The Squeaky Bed" Guide children to use the picture to retell the story. Ask: *What sound scares the girl? Why is the cat in bed with her? What happens next in the story?* Then read the question to children and guide their written responses.

Have partners read their answers to each other. Then have them discuss whether or not the parents were right to bring in the animals, using examples from the story. See Teacher's Edition p. 585 for scaffolded support with this page.

Look at the picture. Read the word. Then read the sentence.

smooth

The lake is smooth today.

soft

The children have soft voices.

pecking

The bird is pecking at the tree.

shouted

The girl shouted to her friends.

COLLABORATE

Vocabulary: *Now, What's that Sound?* Read each word and sentence and have children repeat. Talk about the photos, and explain how the words relate to each image. Provide other contexts for each word. Ask: *What sounds are soft? When do you shout?*

Have children circle the vocabulary word in each sentence. Then have partners work together to write a new sentence for each vocabulary word, and draw pictures to illustrate their ideas. See Teacher's Edition p. 589 for scaffolded support with this page.

Draw and write your ideas for a story.
Ask and answer questions about the story.

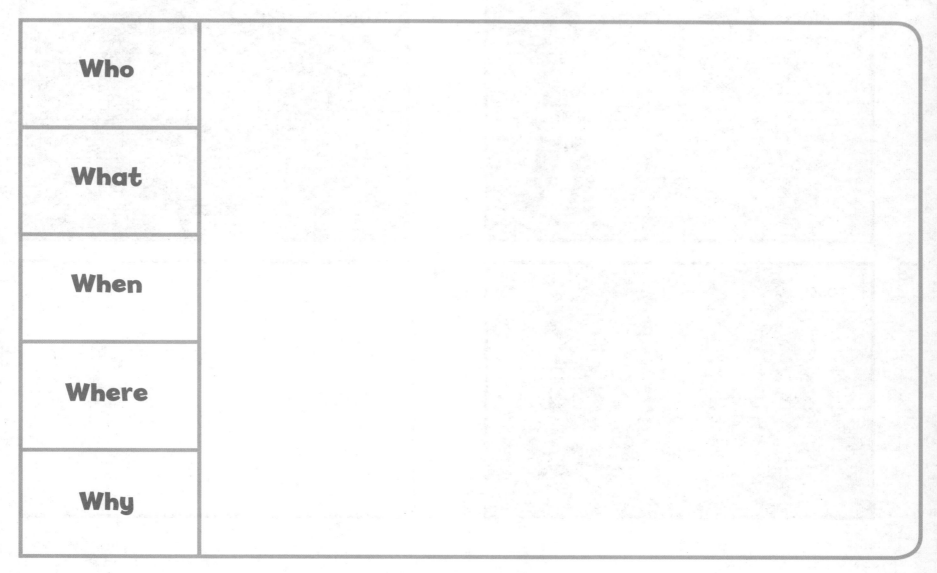

Who	
What	
When	
Where	
Why	

COLLABORATE

Writing Review *Now, What's That Sound?* with children, and introduce the writing prompt: *Write a detective story about a sound. Use the same story structure as* Now, What's That Sound? Have children use the question words to draw and write about their ideas.

Have partners share their drawings and ask and answer questions about their story, such as: *Who is your story about? What is making the sound, and where is that thing?* See Teacher's Edition p. 590 for scaffolded support with this page.

Talk about the pictures. Then, draw.

1.

bounce

2.

whisper

3.

toss

4.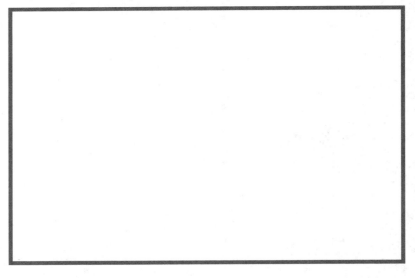

COLLABORATE

Oral Vocabulary: Action Sounds Guide children to talk about what is happening in each picture. Read the labels. Talk about the sounds that each action makes. Then have children draw another action that makes a sound (e.g. *clap, stomp, bang a drum*).

Have partners share their drawings and describe the sound made by the action they drew, using this sentence frame: _____ *makes a* _____ *sound.* See Teacher's Edition p. 592 for scaffolded support with this page.

A Answer the questions.

I. What are Gilbert and Marta looking for?

_____

- -

_____

2. What makes the sounds that they hear?

_____

- -

_____

B Why is it hard for them to find the tap-tap sound? Write about it.

_____

- -

_____

- -

_____

Respond to the Text: *Now, What's that Sound?* Review and retell the story with children. Ask: *Where do the children look for the thing making the sound?* Read the questions and guide children to write their answers.

Have partners read their answers to each other. Have them locate the passage in the text that supports their inference in the last question. See Teacher's Edition p. 595 for scaffolded support with this page.

Listen to the poem. Circle *a, an, this,* and *that.*

A Music Show

A bell goes ring-a-ling.

Then a singer sweetly sings.

That drum goes boom-boom-boom.

You can hear it from across the room.

This music is fast, and then it's slow.

What an excellent music show!

COLLABORATE

Grammar: *A, An, This, That* Read the poem, and discuss its meaning. Have children repeat. Guide children to circle the articles *a, an, this,* and *that* in the poem. Then help children find and underline the nouns that follow the articles.

Have children work with a partner to write new sentences about a show using *a, an, this,* and *that.* Then have partners present their sentences to the group. See Teacher's Edition p. 601 for scaffolded support with this page.

Read the story. Circle words with *ow* and *ou*.

Oh, So Loud!

"What was that sound?" asked Mouse.

"It was nothing," said Cow.

"Was it Bird? He can be loud,"
said Mouse.

"Why is Bird in our barn?" asked Cow.

"I thought you would like my singing,"
said Bird. "Oh, please, can I stay?"

"You may!" said Mouse and Cow.

Fluency Read the story aloud, and discuss its meaning. Reread, and have children echo-read after you. Ask them to listen for changes in your expression. Have children circle words with *ou* and *ow*, and underline the high-frequency words *nothing*, *thought*, and *oh*.

COLLABORATE

Have partners read the story together, taking turns reading every other sentence. Remind them to read with expression, paying attention to questions and exclamations. See Teacher's Edition p. 602 for scaffolded support with this page.

Weekly Concept: Build It!

? Essential Question
How do things get built?

Talk about the picture.
Fix the wall and buildings.

Weekly Concept: Build It! Guide children to name each structure in the picture. Ask: *Which things are not finished or are being repaired?* Have children help the builders by drawing to extend the stone wall, finish the barn, fix the porch, and/or add a new building.

Have partners share their pictures and describe what they added to the scene. Have them discuss what the workers need to do to finish the structures. See Teacher's Edition p. 606 for scaffolded support with this page.

Use the picture to answer the question.

B **Why do the animals build their house near the forest?**

_____

The animals build near the forest because _____

_____

_____ .

COLLABORATE

Respond to the Text: **"The Sheep, the Pig, and the Goose Who Set Up House"** Have children talk about the picture and retell the story. Ask: _What are the pig and the goose doing?_ Then read the question and guide children to use the text to answer.

Have partners share their answers. Then, have them use sequence language to talk about how the animals build their house, using these sentence frames: _First, the animals_ _____. _Next, they_ _____. See Teacher's Edition p. 609 for scaffolded support with this page.

Look at the picture. Read the word. Then read the sentence.

employs

Building employs many workers.

hoist

A crane hoists up building parts.

join

He joins the wood with glue.

protect

Glasses protect her eyes.

COLLABORATE

Vocabulary: *The Joy of a Ship* Read each word and sentence and have children repeat. Talk about the photos, and explain how the words relate to each image. Provide other contexts for each word. Ask: *What protects your head when you ride a bicycle?*

Have children circle the vocabulary word in each sentence. Then have partners write a new sentence for each vocabulary word, and draw pictures to illustrate their ideas. See Teacher's Edition p. 613 for scaffolded support with this page.

Fill in the chart. Then, complete the sentence.

Least Important	Reason

The least important step is _____

_____

because _____ .

COLLABORATE

Writing Review *The Joy of a Ship* with children. Then, introduce the writing prompt: *What do you think is the least important step in building a ship? Why?* Have children draw or write their ideas in the chart. Then guide them to complete the sentence.

Have partners share their ideas and read their sentences to each other. Then have them find the passages in the text that support their opinion. See Teacher's Edition p. 614 for scaffolded support with this page.

Talk about the pictures. Then, draw.

1.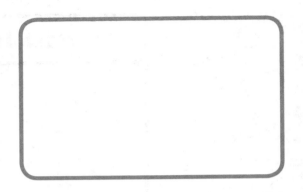

2.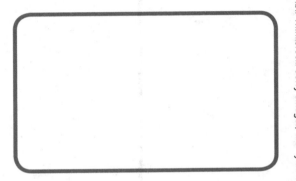

3.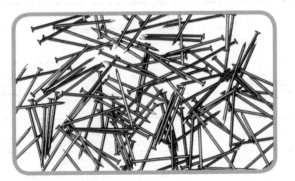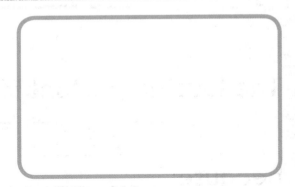

COLLABORATE

Oral Vocabulary **Building Materials** Point to and name the pictures with children. Help children identify the items and the materials: wood, glass, and metal. Have children draw another object made of the same material in each row.

Have partners share their pictures and talk about the material and use of the object they drew, using this sentence frame: *A* _____ *is made from* _____. *It is used to* _____. See Teacher's Edition p. 616 for scaffolded support with this page.

A Answer the questions.

1. What is the first step in building a ship?

_____

- -

_____

2. Why is the metal boiling hot?

_____

- -

_____

B What do workers have to check?
Write about it.

_____

- -

_____

- -

_____

Respond to the Text: *The Joy of a Ship* Review and retell the selection with children. Ask: *What are the steps in building a ship? How do workers protect their hands and heads?* Read the questions, and guide children to write their answers.

COLLABORATE

Have partners read their answers to each other. Have them work together to locate the passages in the text that support their answers. See Teacher's Edition p. 619 for scaffolded support with this page.

Listen to the poem. Circle the prepositions.

An Old House in the Woods

There is an old house in the woods.

Mice hide in the walls.

A snake sleeps under the stairs.

Spiders spin webs near the fireplace.

Birds make nests above the doors.

An owl flies by in the night.

He calls out, "Hoo-Hoo!"

But all is hushed inside the house.

COLLABORATE

Grammar: Prepositions and Prepositional Phrases Read the poem, and discuss its meaning. Have children repeat. Guide children as they draw a line under each prepositional phrase and circle the preposition that begins each phrase.

Have children work with a partner to write new sentences about a house, using prepositional phrases. Have partners present their sentences to the group. See Teacher's Edition p. 625 for scaffolded support with this page.

Read the story. Circle words with *oi* and *oy*.

Let's Build a Bed

"Let's build a bed," Dad said to Roy.
"We will make it strong,
so it will not fall apart."
"This wood is too little," said Roy.
"Is it a toy? Who will sleep in it?"
Dad knew. But Roy did not.
"It is for a baby who will join us soon."
"Oh, wow!" said Roy. "It is a crib!"

COLLABORATE

Fluency Read the story, asking children to listen for changes in your expression. Have children repeat. Discuss the story's meaning. Ask: *What does Dad know?* Have children circle words with *oi* and *oy*, and underline the high-frequency words *build, fall, and knew.*

Have partners read the story to each other. Remind them to read the questions and exclamations with expression. Have partners work together to add one more sentence, with Dad's reply to Roy. See Teacher's Edition p. 626 for scaffolded support with this page.

Together We Can!

The Big Idea

How does teamwork help us?

Weekly Concept: Taking Action

? Essential Question
How can we work together to make our lives better?

Talk about the picture.
Draw another person helping.

Trash

COLLABORATE

Weekly Concept: Taking Action Guide children to discuss how the ...le are working together to make things better. Ask: *What are ...doing? How are they making the park a better place?* ... draw another person helping in the park.

Have children talk with a partner about why a clean park near the river would improve people's lives, using this sentence frame: *A clean park is important because* _____. See Teacher's Edition p. 636 for scaffolded support with this page.

A **Use the picture to answer the question.**

B **How do the mice work together to make their lives better?**

The mice work together by _____

_____

_____

COLLABORATE

Respond to the Text: "The Cat's Bell" Review and retell the story with children. Ask: *What are the mice afraid of? What does the wise old mouse say?* Then read the question and guide children to complete the sentence.

Have partners read their answers to each other. Then have them take turns asking and answering questions about the mice's problem, and how they solve it. See Teacher's Edition p. 639 for scaffolded support with this page.

Look at the picture. Read the word. Then read the sentence.

useful

A rake is a useful tool.

report

She reads her report to the class.

remind

Mom reminds him to be safe.

sketch

The artist makes a sketch.

COLLABORATE

Vocabulary: *Super Tools* Read each word and sentence, and have children repeat. Talk about the photos, and explain how the words relate to each image. Provide other contexts for each word. Ask: *What do grown-ups remind you to do?*

Have children circle the vocabulary word in each sentence. Then have partners write a new sentence for each vocabulary word, and draw pictures to illustrate their ideas. See Teacher's Edition p. 643 for scaffolded support with this page.

Draw or write your ideas. Then, write a letter.

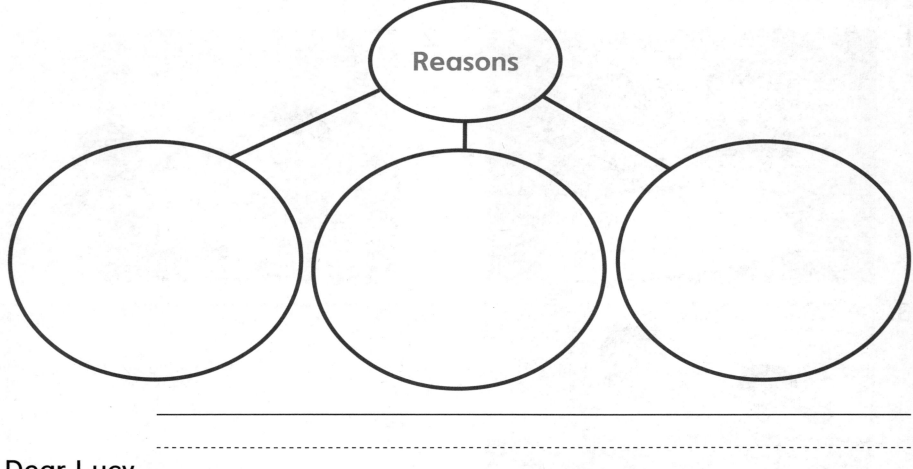

Reasons

_____
- -

Dear Lucy, _____

_____
- -
_____

COLLABORATE

Writing Review *Super Tools* with children. Then, introduce the writing prompt: *Write a letter from the writing tools to Lucy explaining why she needs them.* Guide children to write three reasons why Lucy should use the tools.

Have children begin writing a letter to Lucy on the lines. Then have partners share their ideas and read their writing to each other. Have them act out the role of a writing tool explaining why it is useful. See Teacher's Edition p. 644 for scaffolded support with this page.

Talk about the pictures.
Then, draw one more.

1.

2.

3.

4.

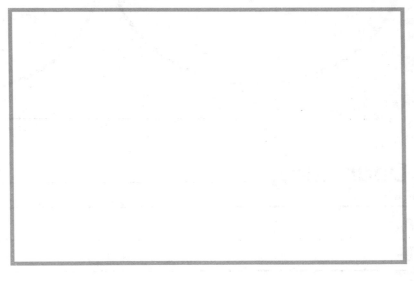

COLLABORATE

Oral Vocabulary: Plan a Food Drive Guide children to describe what is happening in the pictures. Ask: *What are the people doing?* Explain the meanings of *food drive, plan, volunteer,* and *advertise.* Have children draw the final step of the food drive: collecting food.

Have partners discuss why the children are volunteering, and talk about other ways that kids can work together to help others, using the sentence frame: *We can help by _____.* See Teacher's Edition p. 646 for scaffolded support with this page.

216 Unit 6 · Week 1 · Oral Vocabulary

A **Answer the questions.**

I. What new tool does Lucy like to use?

_____

- -

_____

2. Why do the writing tools feel left out?

_____

- -

_____

B **How do the writing tools work together
to fix their problem?**

_____

- -

_____

- -

_____

COLLABORATE

Respond to the Text: *Super Tools* Review and retell the story with
children. Read the questions and guide children to answer them. For
the last question, have children locate the passage in the text that
supports their answer.

Have partners share their answers with each other. Then have them
offer their opinion about which is better, Lucy's new tool or old tools,
and give reasons why. See Teacher's Edition p. 649 for scaffolded
support with this page.

Listen to the poem. Circle the pronouns.

Our Park

Karen and Pedro pick up the trash.
They clean the park in a flash.
Lola paints the old gate.
She fixes it and makes it straight.
Tom cares for the trees.
He waters them and rakes leaves.
You and I must treat the park right.
Together, we'll keep it looking bright.

COLLABORATE

Grammar: Pronouns Read the poem and have children repeat. Discuss the meaning of the poem, and of any unfamiliar words. Then remind children that a pronoun takes the place of a noun. Guide children to find and circle the pronouns.

Have partners use pronouns to write new sentences about taking care of the park. Then have them present their sentences to the group. See Teacher's Edition p. 655 for scaffolded support with this page.

Read the story.
Circle words with *oo*, *u_e*, or *ui*.

The Bake Sale

Each June, we have a bake sale.
We want to help people in need.
We have been busy! My mom and I
brought a cake and a fruit pie.
We have water and juice to sell, too.
We work together to set up at school.
If we sell enough food, we can help
many people!

Bake Sale
Today!

COLLABORATE

Fluency Read the story to children, and discuss its meaning. Then ask volunteers to take turns reading each sentence, copying your phrasing. Have children circle the words with *oo*, *u_e*, or *ui*, and underline the high-frequency words *busy*, *brought*, and *enough*.

Have partners read the story to each other. Remind them to read with expression, and to show emotion when they read the exclamations. See Teacher's Edition p. 656 for scaffolded support with this page.

Weekly Concept: My Team

? Essential Question
Who helps you?

Talk about the picture.
Circle the people who are helping.

COLLABORATE

Weekly Concept: My Team Guide children to talk about the picture. Ask: *What are the people doing? Who is getting help? Who are the helpers and how are they helping?* Have children circle the people who are helping.

Have partners name the people who help them and explain how they help, using this sentence frame: _____ *helps me to* _____. See Teacher's Edition p. 660 for scaffolded support with this page.

A Use the picture to answer the question.

B Choose one of Anansi's sons.
How does he help Anansi?

_____

Anansi's son helps him by _____

_____

_____

COLLABORATE

Respond to the Text: "Anansi's Sons" Review and retell the story with children. Ask: *How do each of Anansi's sons help their father?* Guide children to read the question and complete the sentence.

Have partners read their answers to each other. Then have them take turns asking and answering questions about each of Anansi's sons. See Teacher's Edition p. 663 for scaffolded support with this page.

**Look at the picture. Read the word.
Then read the sentence.**

subject

He picks a subject to read about.

checkup

The dog needs a checkup.

include

Breakfast can include fruit.

safety

Follow all safety rules and signs.

COLLABORATE

Vocabulary: *All Kinds of Helpers* Read each word and sentence, and have children repeat. Talk about the photos, and explain how the words relate to each image. Provide other contexts for each word. Ask: *What is your favorite subject in school?*

Have children circle the vocabulary word in each sentence. Then have partners write a new sentence for each vocabulary word, and draw pictures to illustrate their ideas. See Teacher's Edition p. 667 for scaffolded support with this page.

Draw or write your ideas. Then, write a sentence.

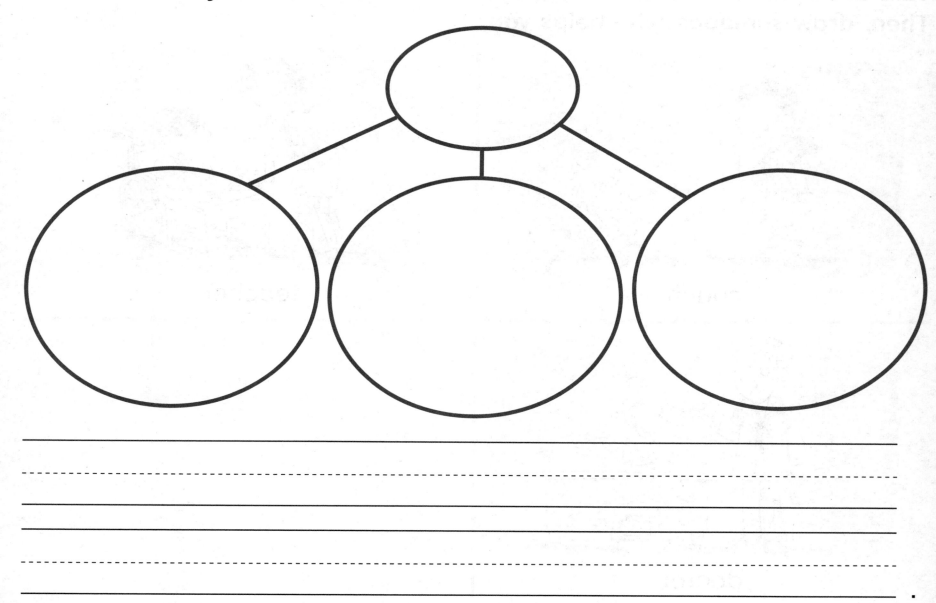

_____

- -

_____

- -

_____ .

COLLABORATE

Writing Review *All Kinds of Helpers* with children. Then, introduce the writing prompt: *Write about a group of helpers in your community.* Guide children to fill in the web with a type of helper in the top oval, and three ways they help in the other ovals.

Have children write a sentence about the helpers they chose. Then have partners share their sentences, and tell a story about a helper from the group that they chose. See Teacher's Edition p. 668 for scaffolded support with this page.

Talk about the pictures.
Then, draw someone who helps you.

coach

teacher

doctor

COLLABORATE

Oral Vocabulary: Helpers Guide children to point to each picture and read the label. Ask: *Who needs help here? Who is helping? How are they helping?* Then have children draw a picture of a special helper in their life.

Have partners share their drawings and talk about the person who helps them. Then have them offer opinions about the most helpful person in their life, providing reasons why. See Teacher's Edition p. 670 for scaffolded support with this page.

A Answer the questions.

1. Who helps us at home?

_____

- -

_____

2. Who helps us in the community?

_____

- -

_____

B Choose one helper in the book.
Write about how that person helps.

_____

- -

_____

- -

_____

COLLABORATE

_____

Respond to the Text: **All Kinds of Helpers** Review the selection with children. Have children name people who help them. Then, read the questions and guide children's answers. For the last question, have children locate the passage in the text that supports their answer.

Have partners read their answers to each other. Then have them act out the roles of a helper from the story, and a person they help. See Teacher's Edition p. 673 for scaffolded support with this page.

Masterfile

A Listen to the rhyme.
Circle the possessive pronouns.

Teamwork

Mark does his math.

Nora does her science.

Homework can be a hard task.

Mark helps with her science.

Nora helps with his math.

This way, homework goes fast!

B Write the possessive pronoun.

_____

Mark's book   _____ book

_____

Nora's pen   _____ pen

COLLABORATE

Grammar: **Possessive Pronouns** Read the rhyme and have children repeat. Guide children to circle the possessive pronouns in the poem, and name more, such as *my, your, our* and *their*. Then have children write the possessive pronoun that completes each phrase.

Guide partners to reread the poem and discuss its meaning. Then have them work together to write new sentences that use possessive pronouns, and present their sentences to the group. See Teacher's Edition p. 679 for scaffolded support with this page.

Read the story. Circle words with *aw* and *al*.

My Baby Brother

I love my baby brother!
I take good care of him and
teach him lots of things.
My brother can crawl very fast.
Soon, I will help him learn to walk.
My mother and father say
I'm a great helper!

COLLABORATE

Fluency Read the story to children, and discuss its meaning. Then have volunteers take turns reading each sentence, copying your expression. Have children circle words with *aw* and *al*, and underline the high-frequency words *brother, love, mother*, and *father*.

Have partners take turns reading the story to each other. Remind them to read with expression, and to pause at end punctuation. See Teacher's Edition p. 680 for scaffolded support with this page.

Essential Question
How can weather affect us?

Talk about the pictures.
Circle the differences.

COLLABORATE

Weekly Concept: Weather Together Guide children to name and describe the different kinds of weather in each picture. Ask: *What kind of weather is this? How does this kind of weather affect people?* Have children circle and name differences between the two pictures.

Ask partners to name their favorite kind of weather. Have them support their opinions using this sentence frame: *I like _____ because _____.* See Teacher's Edition p. 684 for scaffolded support with this page.

A **Use the picture to answer the question.**

B **Why does the corn pop and make a popcorn blizzard?**

_____

The corn pops because _____

_____

_____ .

COLLABORATE

Respond to the Text: "Paul Bunyan and the Popcorn Blizzard"
Have children discuss the unique characteristics of Paul Bunyan. Ask:
What kinds of things is Paul Bunyan able to do? Then guide children
to read the question and complete the sentence.

Have partners read their answers to each other. Then have them
retell and act out a scene from the story. See Teacher's Edition p. 687
for scaffolded support with this page.

Look at the picture. Read the word. Then read the sentence.

coat

They coat the fence with paint.

sparkle

The jewels sparkle in the light.

advise

The coach advises a player.

cozy

He has a warm, cozy blanket.

COLLABORATE

Vocabulary: *Wrapped in Ice* Read each word and sentence, and have children repeat. Talk about the photos, and explain how the words relate to each image. Provide other contexts for each word. Ask: *What would you coat with frosting? Who advises you?*

Have children circle the vocabulary word in each sentence. Then have partners write a new sentence for each vocabulary word, and draw pictures to illustrate their ideas. See Teacher's Edition p. 691 for scaffolded support with this page.

Draw or write your ideas in the web.
Then, complete the sentence.

what
people do

The neighbors _____

_____

_____

_____ .

Writing Review *Wrapped in Ice* with children. Then introduce the writing prompt: *How do the people in the town react to the weather in* Wrapped in Ice? Have children fill in the web with details that show what the people do because of the ice storm.

Guide children to complete the sentence to tell what the neighbors do. Then have partners read their sentences to each other, and show where they found the details in the text. See Teacher's Edition p. 692 for scaffolded support with this page.

Talk about the pictures.
Then, draw your own picture.

Oral Vocabulary: Dress for the Weather Guide children to name the clothing and accessories, and describe the weather for which each is appropriate. Then have children draw themselves wearing appropriate clothing in a weather scene of their choice.

Have children share their drawings with a partner and describe the weather and clothing they drew, using this sentence frame: *The weather is _____ so I am wearing _____.* See Teacher's Edition p. 694 for scaffolded support with this page.

A Answer the questions.

1. What does Kim see outside the window?

_____

- -

_____

2. Why does the power go out?

_____

- -

_____

B What do Kim and her mom do during the storm?

_____

- -

_____

- -

_____

COLLABORATE

Respond to the Text: *Wrapped in Ice* Review and retell the story with children. Then read the questions and guide children to answer them. For the last question, ask children to locate the passage in the text that supports their answer.

Have partners read their answers to each other. Then guide them to expand the story by telling what they think happens after the lights come on. Have them present their new ending to the group. See Teacher's Edition p. 697 for scaffolded support with this page.

Listen to the poem. Circle special pronouns.

Bring Back the Sun

Everyone likes a sunny day,
but nobody likes the rain.
When it rains there's nothing
for us to play.
So we sit inside and then we say:
"Rain, rain go away!
Somebody bring back
the sun today!"

Grammar: Special Pronouns Read the poem, and discuss its
meaning. Read the poem again, pointing out and explaining the
special pronouns *everyone, nobody, nothing,* and *somebody.* Then
have children circle those pronouns.

COLLABORATE

Have partners work together to write new sentences about what
people like to do on sunny days, using the special pronouns *everyone*
or *anyone.* See Teacher's Edition p. 703 for scaffolded support with
this page.

Read the letter. Circle words with silent letters.

Summer at Grandma's

Dear Maria,

I'm having fun at Grandma's.
She taught me how to knit!
I know many children here.
There are lots of bees and gnats.
I was stung by a bee on my knee!
Don't worry, I'm fine.
I'll be home next month. How have
you been? Write soon!

Love,
Lucy

Fluency Read the letter to children, and explain any unfamiliar vocabulary. Then have children echo-read after you, copying your phrasing. Have children circle words with the silent letters *wr, kn,* and *gn,* and underline the words *children, month,* and *been.*

Have partners take turns reading the letter to each other. Remind them to read with expression, and to pause at commas and at end punctuation. See Teacher's Edition p. 704 for scaffolded support with this page.

Weekly Concept: Sharing Traditions

? Essential Question
What traditions do you know about?

Talk about the picture.
Draw food from your family's tradition.

COLLABORATE

Weekly Concept: Sharing Traditions Guide children to discuss the scene. Ask: *What is the father doing? What special foods are traditional in your family? Who could teach you how to make them?* Have children draw a traditional food from their family on the plate.

Have partners name and describe the traditional food they drew and give their opinion of it, using these sentence frames: *In my family, we eat _____. I like/ don't like it because _____.* See Teacher's Edition p. 708 for scaffolded support with this page.

A Use the pictures to answer the question.

B Why is dancing an important tradition in many cultures?

_____

- -

Dancing is important because _____

- -

_____ .

COLLABORATE

Respond to the Text: "Let's Dance!" Review the selection with children. Have them talk about the people in each picture. Ask: *How are these dances alike and different?* Then guide children to answer the question and complete the sentence.

Have partners read their answers to each other. Then have them take turns asking and answering questions about the dances described in the selection. See Teacher's Edition p. 711 for scaffolded support with this page.

(l) Owen Franken/Corbis; (r) Photo Researchers/Getty Images

Look at the picture. Read the word. Then read the sentence.

picnic

We eat outside at a picnic.

strikes

The boy strikes the ball.

shriek

The baby shrieks when tickled.

scramble

They scramble to be first in line.

COLLABORATE

Vocabulary: *A Spring Birthday* Read each word and sentence, and have children repeat. Talk about the photos, and explain how the words relate to each image. Provide other contexts for each word. Ask: *What do you eat at a picnic? When would you shriek?*

Have children circle the vocabulary word in each sentence. Then have partners write a new sentence for each vocabulary word, and draw pictures to illustrate their ideas. See Teacher's Edition p. 715 for scaffolded support with this page.

Draw your ideas. Then, complete the sentence.

I want to _____

_____

_____ .

COLLABORATE

Writing Review *A Spring Birthday* with children. Then introduce the writing prompt: *Write a letter from Marco to his parents explaining why he wants to start a new tradition. Describe what the new tradition might be.*

Have children draw a picture of Marco's new tradition, and complete the sentence. Then have partners compose their letters orally. Remind them that a letter contains a greeting and a closing. See Teacher's Edition p. 716 for scaffolded support with this page.

Draw a family tradition.
Then, talk about it.

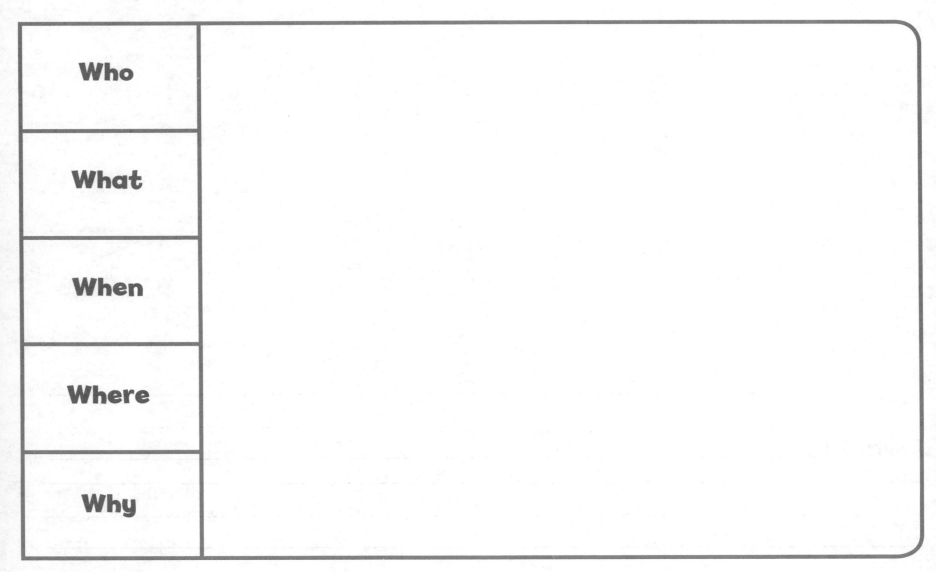

Who	
What	
When	
Where	
Why	

COLLABORATE

Oral Vocabulary: Family Traditions Explain that family traditions are special things that families do together. Ask: *What traditions do you have in your family?* Have children draw a favorite family tradition.

Have partners share their drawings. Then have them take turns asking and answering the five "W" questions about each other's pictures. See Teacher's Edition p. 718 for scaffolded support with this page.

A Answer the questions.

1. Why does Marco want a special dinner?

_____

- -

_____

2. What does Dad suggest instead?

_____

- -

_____

B How does Marco blend old and new ideas to make a new tradition?

_____

- -

_____

- -

_____

COLLABORATE

Respond to the Text: *A Spring Birthday* Review the story with children. Read the questions and guide children to answer them. For the last question, ask children to locate the passage in the text that supports their answer.

Have partners read their answers to each other. Then have them offer opinions about which birthday tradition they like better, the old or the new, and give reasons why. See Teacher's Edition p. 721 for scaffolded support with this page.

A Listen to the riddle. Circle *I* and *me*.

What Am I?

You can touch me,
but I do not like pins.
You can toss me,
but I am not a ball.
You can find me at a party,
but I cannot sing.

B Complete each sentence with *I* or *me*.

_____

_____ like parties.

_____

My friend invited _____ to a party.

COLLABORATE

Grammar: *I and Me* Read the riddle, and explain its meaning. Then have children echo-read after you. Have children clap when they hear *I* or *me*, and circle those words. Ask children to solve the riddle. Then have them complete each sentence with *I* or *me*.

Have partners work together to write another clue to extend the riddle, using the pronouns *I* and *me*. Then have them present their new clue to the group. See Teacher's Edition p. 727 for scaffolded support with this page.

Read the story. Circle words with blends.

Summer Picnic

Each summer, my sister and I
walk down to the stream.
We have a picnic there.
Before we eat, we take turns on
the tire swing. I push her, and she
jumps off the front of the swing.
Splish! Splash! What fun!
We swim and throw a ball.
Then we are ready to eat!

COLLABORATE

Fluency Read the story to children, and discuss its meaning. Then have children echo-read after you. Guide children to circle words with three letter blends. Then have them underline the high-frequency words *before, push,* and *front.*

Have partners take turns reading the story to each other until they can read it fluently. Remind them to show emotion when reading exclamations. See Teacher's Edition p. 728 for scaffolded support with this page.

Weekly Concept: Celebrate America!

Talk about the picture.
Draw yourself celebrating.

Happy 4th of July!

COLLABORATE

Weekly Concept: Celebrate America! Guide children to name and talk about what is happening in the scene. Explain the word *celebration,* and discuss why we celebrate our country. Have children draw themselves marching in the parade.

Have partners share their drawings and explain what they are doing in the parade. Then have them talk about their own Fourth of July or parade experiences. See Teacher's Edition p. 732 for scaffolded support with this page.

A Use the pictures to answer the question.

B How is today's flag different from the old U.S. flag?

_____
- -

Today's flag _____
_____
- -
_____ .

COLLABORATE

Respond to the Text: "Celebrate the Flag" Review the selection with children. Ask: *What ideas does our flag represent? What do the stars and stripes mean?* Then guide children to answer the question and complete the sentence.

Have partners read their answers to each other. Then have them work together to make a list of three things they learned about the U.S. flag from the selection. See Teacher's Edition p. 735 for scaffolded support with this page.

Look at the picture. Read the word. Then read the sentence.

crops

Farmers grow crops, like lettuce.

fair

The fair is a fun place to visit.

feast

We have a feast on holidays.

compost

We use compost in our garden.

COLLABORATE

Vocabulary: *Share the Harvest and Give Thanks* Read each word and sentence, and have children repeat. Talk about the photos, and explain how the words relate to each image. Provide other contexts for each word. Ask: *When does your family have a feast?*

Have children circle the vocabulary word in each sentence. Then have partners write a new sentence for each vocabulary word, and draw pictures to illustrate their ideas. See Teacher's Edition p. 739 for scaffolded support with this page.

Draw or write your ideas.
Then, complete the sentence.

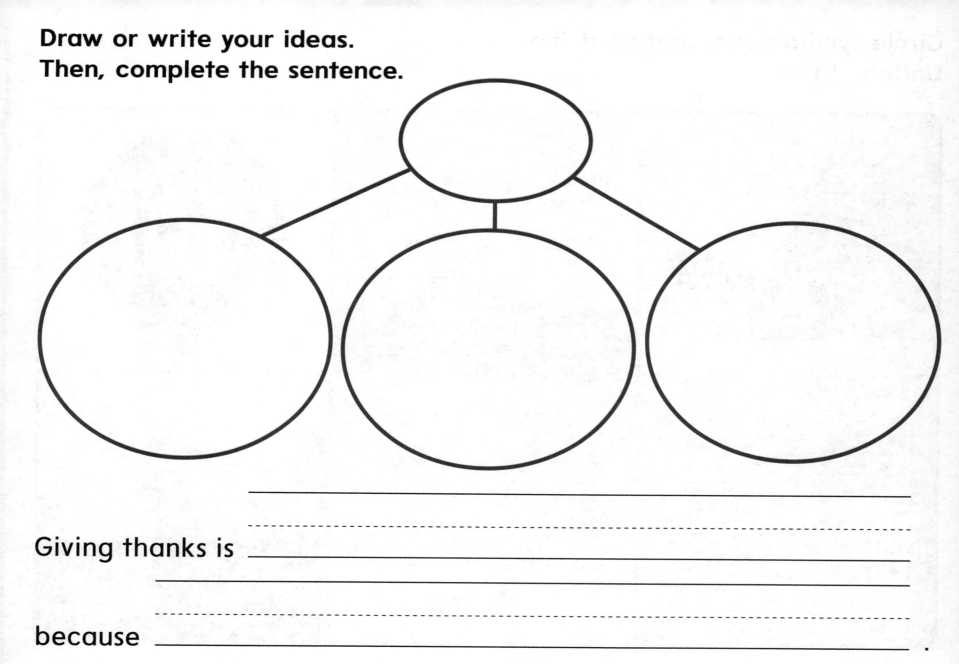

Giving thanks is _____

_____

because _____ .

COLLABORATE

Writing Review *Share the Harvest and Give Thanks*. Then introduce the writing prompt: *Do you think it is important or not important to give thanks for a harvest? Why?* Have children write *important* or *not important* in the top oval, and then provide three reasons.

Guide children to complete the sentence. Then have partners read their completed sentences to each other, and try to persuade each other why their position is correct. See Teacher's Edition p. 740 for scaffolded support with this page.

Circle symbols that represent the United States.

COLLABORATE

Oral Vocabulary: National Symbols Guide children to name each item pictured. Explain that national symbols represent larger ideas about our country. Have children circle the pictures that symbolize the United States, and discuss what each symbol represents.

Have partners choose one national symbol and talk together about what it means to them, using this sentence frame: *When I see _____, it makes me think _____.* See Teacher's Edition p. 742 for scaffolded support with this page.

A Answer the questions.

1. What are some harvest foods?

_____

- -

_____

2. Who first celebrated Thanksgiving?

_____

- -

_____

B How do people celebrate Thanksgiving? Write about it.

_____

- -

_____

- -

_____

COLLABORATE

Respond to the Text: ***Share the Harvest and Give Thanks*** Review the selection with children. Ask: *What is a harvest? Why is it important?* Guide children to answer the questions. For the last question, have them locate text evidence to support their answers.

Have partners read their answers to each other. Then have them offer opinions about their favorite harvest tradition, and explain why. See Teacher's Edition p. 745 for scaffolded support with this page.

A Listen to the poem.
Circle the adverbs.

Flying Proudly

We raise the flag slowly.

We sing the anthem loudly.

The stars shine brightly.

We salute the flag proudly.

B Write two adverbs from the poem.

_____   _____

- - - - - - - - - - - - - - - - -   - - - - - - - - - - - - - - - - -

_____   _____

COLLABORATE

Grammar: Adverbs That Tell How Read the poem, and explain its meaning. Reread, and have children repeat. Remind children that adverbs are words that tell how something happened. Have children circle the adverbs, and write two of them on the lines.

Have partners work together to write a new sentence for the poem that tells how the flag is lowered at night, using an adverb. Then have them present their new sentence to the group. See Teacher's Edition p. 751 for scaffolded support with this page.

Read the story.
Circle words with *are*, *air*, and *ear*.

A Trip to the Fair

"I have a surprise," said Clare.

"We are going to the fair!"

"Fairs are my favorite!" I said.

At the fair, we saw a bear!

I smelled popcorn in the air.

I got some for us to share.

"Let's go on a few rides," I said.

"What fun!" said Clare.

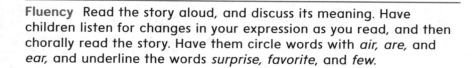

Fluency Read the story aloud, and discuss its meaning. Have children listen for changes in your expression as you read, and then chorally read the story. Have them circle words with *air*, *are*, and *ear*, and underline the words *surprise*, *favorite*, and *few*.

COLLABORATE

Have partners take turns reading the story to each other. Remind them to pay attention to end punctuation, and to read with expression. See Teacher's Edition p. 752 for scaffolded support with this page.

The Alphabet

A: Apple – Stockdisc/PunchStock; B: Bat – CrackerClips/iStock/Getty Images Plus/Getty Images; C: Camel – Photokanok/iStock/Getty Images Plus/Getty Images; D: Dolphin – imagebroker/Alamy;
E: Egg – Pixtal/age footstock; F: Fire – Comstock Images/Alamy; G: Guitar – Jules Frazier/Photodisc/Getty Images; H: Hippo – subinpumsom/iStock/Getty Images Plus/Getty Images; I: Insect – Ingram
Publishing/Fotosearch; J: Jump – Photodisc/Getty Images; K: Koala – ©Al Franklin/Corbis; L: Lemon – C Squared Studios/Photodisc/Getty Images; M: Map – McGraw-Hill Education; N: Nest – Siede Preis/
Photodisc/Getty Images; O: Octopus – Photographers Choice RF/SuperStock; P: Piano – Ingram Publishing/Alamy; Q: Queen – Joshua Ets-Hokin/Photodisc/Getty Images; R: Rose – ranasu/iStock/Getty Images
Plus/Getty Images; S: Sun – 97/E+/Getty Images; T: Turtle – Ingram Publishing; U: Umbrella – Stockbyte/Getty Images; V: Volcano – Westend6l/Getty Images; W: Window – emarto/iStock/Getty Images Plus/
Getty Images; X: Box – C Squared Studios/Photodisc/Getty Images; Y: Yo-Yo – D. Hurst/Alamy; Z: Zipper – Image State/Alamy

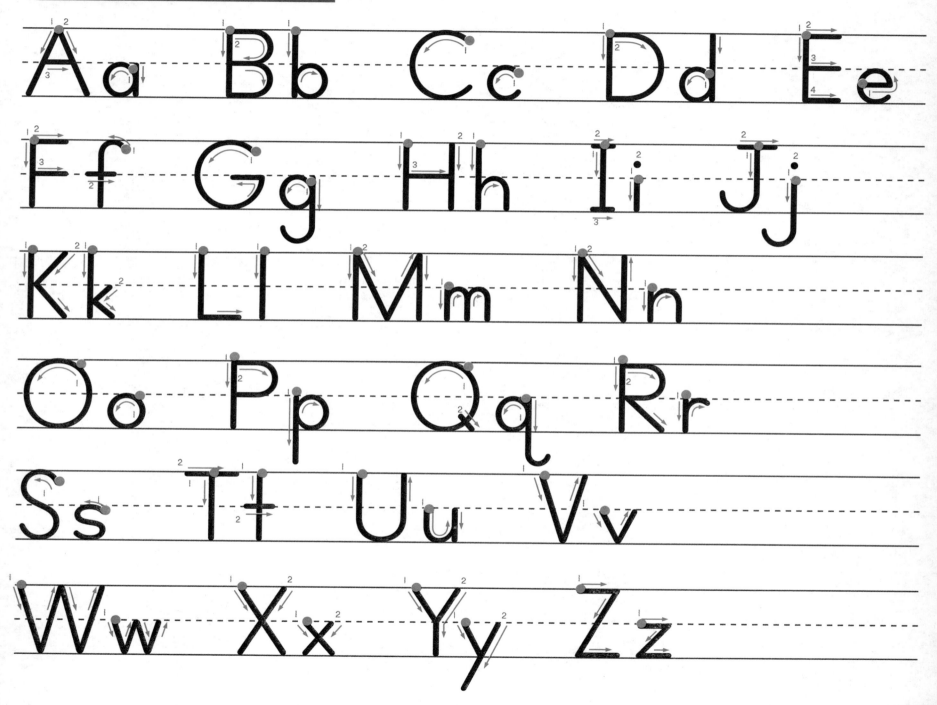